PATHWAYS

SECOND EDITION

1

Reading, Writing, and Critical Thinking

MARI VARGO

LAURIE BLASS

Australia • Brazil • Mexico • Singapore • United Kingdom • United States

Pathways
Reading, Writing, and Critical Thinking 1,
Second Edition

Mari Vargo and Laurie Blass

Publisher: Andrew Robinson

Executive Editor: Sean Bermingham

Development Editor: Melissa Pang

Director of Global Marketing: Ian Martin

Product Marketing Manager: Tracy Bailie

Media Researcher: Leila Hishmeh

IP Analyst: Michelle McKenna

IP Project Manager: Carissa Poweleit

Senior Director of Production:
   Michael Burggren

Senior Production Controller: Tan Jin Hock

Manufacturing Planner: Mary Beth
   Hennebury

Art Director: Brenda Carmichael

Compositor: MPS North America LLC

Cover Photo: The Milky Way shines
   above sequoias in Yosemite National
   Park, USA: © Babak Tafreshi/National
   Geographic Creative

For product information and technology assistance, contact us at
Cengage Learning Customer & Sales Support, cengage.com/contact
For permission to use material from this text or product,
submit all requests online at **cengage.com/permissions**
Further permissions questions can be emailed to
permissionrequest@cengage.com

Student Book:
ISBN-13: 978-1-337-40776-2

Student Book with Online Workbook:
ISBN-13: 978-1-337-62510-4

National Geographic Learning
20 Channel Center Street
Boston, MA 02210
USA

National Geographic Learning, a Cengage Learning Company, has a mission to bring the world to the classroom and the classroom to life. With our English language programs, students learn about their world by experiencing it. Through our partnerships with National Geographic and TED Talks, they develop the language and skills they need to be successful global citizens and leaders.

Locate your local office at **international.cengage.com/region**

Visit National Geographic Learning online at **NGL.Cengage.com/ELT**
Visit our corporate website at **www.cengage.com**

Printed in China

Print Number: 03 Print Year: 2018

Contents

Scope and Sequence

Critical Thinking	Writing	Vocabulary Extension
Focus Inferring Meaning Applying, Synthesizing, Reflecting	**Skill Focus** Writing Good Sentences **Language for Writing** Using Simple Present Tense **Writing Goal** Writing sentences to describe daily activities	**Word Forms** Verbs and Nouns **Word Partners** verb + *time*
Focus Identifying Evidence Evaluating, Inferring, Applying	**Skill Focus** Ordering Ideas **Language for Writing** Using *want* and *need* **Writing Goal** Writing sentences about a personal learning goal	**Word Link** *in-* and *im-* **Word Partners** verb + *up*
Focus Relating Ideas Reflecting	**Skill Focus** Writing Paragraphs and Topic Sentences **Language for Writing** Connecting Ideas **Writing Goal** Writing a paragraph about the effectiveness of an ad	**Word Partners** verb + *control* **Word Partners** *natural* + noun
Focus Analyzing Problems and Solutions Synthesizing, Applying, Inferring Meaning	**Skill Focus** Using Supporting Sentences **Language for Writing** Stating Problems and Proposing Solutions **Writing Goal** Writing a paragraph about possible solutions to an environmental issue	**Word Link** *re-* **Word Partners** Antonyms
Focus Justifying Your Opinion	**Skill Focus** Paraphrasing Using Synonyms **Language for Writing** Giving Reasons **Writing Goal** Writing a paragraph explaining why people enjoy sharing pictures of food	**Word Forms** Words as Nouns and Verbs **Word Forms** Changing Adjectives into Adverbs

Scope and Sequence

Critical Thinking	Writing	Vocabulary Extension
Focus Inferring Attitude Applying, Synthesizing, Justifying Your Opinion	**Skill Focus** Using Pronouns to Avoid Repetition **Language for Writing** Using *And*, *But*, and *So* **Writing Goal** Writing a paragraph about a typical day in the year 2050	**Word Link** *-able* **Word Forms** Changing Verbs into Nouns
Focus Understanding Analogies Applying, Analyzing	**Skill Focus** Introducing Examples **Language for Writing** Expressing Interests and Desires **Writing Goal** Writing a paragraph about a place worth exploring	**Word Forms** Adjectives and Nouns for Measurement **Word Partners** *run* + adverb/preposition
Focus Interpreting Idiomatic Language Inferring Meaning, Synthesizing, Evaluating	**Skill Focus** Planning a Narrative Paragraph **Language for Writing** Using Time Expressions **Writing Goal** Writing a paragraph about the life of a musician or performer	**Word Link** *dis-* **Word Forms** Changing Adjectives into Nouns
Focus Inferring Opinion Reflecting, Applying	**Skill Focus** Writing a Comparison Paragraph **Language for Writing** Making Comparisons **Writing Goal** Writing a paragraph comparing the behavior of two different animals	**Word Link** *-er* and *-or* **Word Forms** Homonyms
Focus Evaluating Using Criteria Analyzing, Applying	**Skill Focus** Writing an Opinion Paragraph **Language for Writing** Describing Spatial Relationships Describing Emotions **Writing Goal** Writing a paragraph to explain why a photograph is good	**Word Link** *vis* **Word Forms** Changing Verbs into Adjectives

Pathways Reading, Writing, and Critical Thinking, Second Edition uses National Geographic stories, photos, video, and infographics to bring the world to the classroom. Authentic, relevant content and carefully sequenced lessons engage learners while equipping them with the skills needed for academic success. Each level of the second edition features **NEW** and **UPDATED** content.

Academic skills are clearly ▸ labeled at the beginning of each unit.

ACADEMIC SKILLS

READING	Identifying main ideas of paragraphs
WRITING	Ordering ideas
GRAMMAR	Using *want* and *need*
CRITICAL THINKING	Identifying evidence

NEW Reading passages ▸ incorporate a variety of text types, charts, and infographics to inform and inspire learners.

Explicit reading skill instruction ▸ includes main ideas, details, inference, prediction, gist, note-taking, sequencing, and vocabulary development.

▾ **Critical thinking activities** are integrated throughout each unit, and help develop learner independence.

CRITICAL THINKING **Inferring** a writer's **attitude** means thinking about how they feel about the subject. Ask yourself: Is the author generally positive or negative? What clues indicate the author's attitude?

Video

National Geographic Explorer
Martin Edström and an assistant
photographer in Son Doong cave

THE LOST WORLD

BEFORE VIEWING

A Work with a partner. Read the title and look at the photo. How big do you think the cave is? Use an analogy to describe your ideas.

B Read the information about Son Doong. Then answer the questions.

At more than five kilometers long, Son Doong is one of the largest caves in the world. The cave—located in Vietnam—was created millions of years ago when river water caused the rock under the mountain to become soft and fall apart. A man called Ho Khanh discovered Son Doong in 1991, but he didn't know how to enter it. As a result, the cave remained a mystery. In 2009, a team of British cavers began to explore Son Doong with the help of Ho Khanh. A year later, a different team of cavers visited, and became the first people to explore the entire length of the cave.

1. Where is the cave? _____

2. Is the cave natural or man-made? _____

3. Who were the first people to enter the cave? _____

4. What do you think explorers might find in the cave? _____

_____

◀ **UPDATED *Video* sections** use National Geographic video clips to provide a bridge between Readings 1 and 2, and to give learners ideas and language for the unit's writing task.

◀ **NEW** An additional short reading passage provides integrated skills practice.

Reading 1

PREPARING TO READ

BUILDING VOCABULARY **A** The words and phrases in blue below are used in the reading passage on pages 5–6. Complete each sentence with the correct word or phrase.

| project take care of produce team normal arrive extraordinary |

1. If something is _____ it is wonderful and very rare.

2. When you _____ somewhere, you get there from somewhere else.

3. A _____ is a group of people who work together, for example, on a _____.

4. If something is _____ it is usual and not very special.

5. When you _____ people, you make sure they have everything they need.

6. When you _____ something, you make it.

USING VOCABULARY **B** Discuss these questions with a partner.

1. How do you usually **communicate** with your friends and family?

2. What is one thing that you do on a **normal** day?

BRAINSTORMING **C** List things that you think most people around the world do every day. Share your ideas with a partner.

brush teeth

daily activities

SCANNING/ PREDICTING **D** Scan for the numbers in the first paragraph. Then look at the words around them. What do you think the passage is about? Check your answer as you read.

a. a day in the life of a movie director

b. a very unusual day on our planet

c. a movie about one day on Earth

4 UNIT 1

▲ **Key academic and thematic vocabulary** is practiced, and expanded throughout each unit.

VOCABULARY EXTENSION UNIT 1

WORD FORMS Verbs and Nouns

Some verbs ending in -*t* and -*s* can be made into nouns by adding -*ion* to the end of the word. For verbs ending in -*e*, spell the noun without the -*e*.	**VERB**	**NOUN**
	communicate	communication
	connect	connection
	discuss	discussion

A Complete each sentence with the correct verb or noun form of the words below.

| communicate connect contribute discuss populate |

1. We should have a meeting to _____ our project.

2. The _____ of the Earth is now over seven billion people.

3. Today, text messaging is one of the most popular forms of _____.

4. Anyone can upload a video to YouTube as long as they have an Internet _____.

5. To make the *Life in a Day* movie, the team asked people to _____ a video of their daily life.

WORD PARTNERS verb + *time*

Collocations are words that often go together, such as *spend time*. Some collocations are in the verb + noun form. Below are definitions for common collocations with the noun *time*.

have time: to be free to do something
spend time: to use time to do something
waste time: to use time without purpose
save time: to reduce the amount of time it takes to do something
kill time: to do something while waiting for something else to happen

B Complete each sentence with the correct form of the collocations from the box above.

1. The deadline for this project is tomorrow, so we can't _____ chatting.

2. I am really busy at the moment, so I don't _____ to take on an additional project.

3. I was early for the meeting, so I _____ by replying to emails.

4. I _____ when I leave work early. The traffic is lighter and I get home more quickly.

5. It is hard to balance work and family, but I try to _____ with my kids every day.

▲ **NEW Vocabulary extension activities** cover word forms, collocations, affixes, phrasal verbs, and more, to boost learners' reading and writing fluency.

Writing Skills Practice

Pathways' approach to writing guides students through the writing process and develops learners' confidence in planning, drafting, revising, and editing.

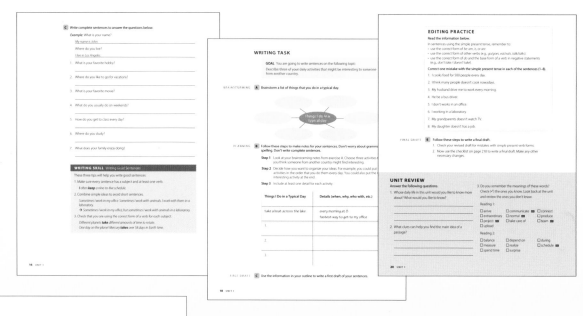

Writing Goals and **Language for Writing** ▶ sections provide the focus and scaffolding needed for learners to become successful writers.

WRITING TASK

GOAL You are going to write sentences on the following topic:
Describe three of your daily activities that might be interesting to someone from another country.

LANGUAGE FOR WRITING Simple Present Tense

Use the simple present for habits and daily routines.
*Sometimes I **work** in my office.*
*I **don't have** classes on Tuesdays.*
*Every day, more than eight million people **travel** by plane.*

Also use the simple present for facts and general statements about people a
*A single day **is** 24 hours long.*
*Christine Lee **studies** the skeletons of ancient humans.*
*It **takes** the Earth 24 hours to make one rotation.*
*In northern Finland the sun **doesn't set** in the summer.*

Note: To create the negative form, add *doesn't* or *don't* to the base verb.

▼ An **online workbook**, powered by MyELT, includes video clips and automatically graded activities for learners to practice the skills taught in the Student Books.

UPDATED Revising ▶ **Practice** sections incorporate realistic model paragraphs and help learners refine their writing.

NEW Guided online writing ▶ **practice** provides reinforcement and consolidation of language skills, helping learners to become stronger and more confident writers.

LIFE IN A DAY 1

A busy street in Karachi, Pakistan

ACADEMIC SKILLS

READING	Skimming for gist
WRITING	Writing good sentences
GRAMMAR	Simple present tense
CRITICAL THINKING	Inferring meaning

THINK AND DISCUSS

1 Which day of the week do you like best? Which day do you like least? Why?

2 What is one thing you enjoy doing every day? Why?

A Read the information on these pages and answer the questions.

1. How much does the world's population increase in a day? How many people fly to a different place? How many people visit Facebook?

2. Do you use the Internet every day? What kinds of things do you use it for?

B Match the correct form of the words in blue to their definitions.

_____ (v) to link or bring together

_____ (v) to share information by speaking, writing etc.

_____ (v) to make available on the Internet

IN ONE DAY ON PLANET EARTH . . .

▸ The world's population grows by about **200,000** people.

▸ More than **8,000,000** people travel by plane.

▸ About **200,000** people move into cities.

▸ More than **4,000,000,000** people communicate with others through their cell phones.

▸ Social media website Facebook connects over **1,000,000,000** people.

▸ People upload more than **576,000** hours of video to YouTube.

1,000 = one thousand   1,000,000 = one million   1,000,000,000 = one billion

Cities and communication lines stand out in this image of planet Earth.

Reading 1

PREPARING TO READ

BUILDING
VOCABULARY

A The words and phrases in **blue** below are used in the reading passage on pages 5–6. Complete each sentence with the correct word or phrase.

> project   take care of   produce   team   normal   arrive   extraordinary

1. If something is _____, it is wonderful and very rare.

2. When you _____ somewhere, you get there from somewhere else.

3. A _____ is a group of people who work together, for example, on a _____.

4. If something is _____, it is usual and not very special.

5. When you _____ people, you make sure they have everything they need.

6. When you _____ something, you make it.

USING
VOCABULARY

B Discuss these questions with a partner.

1. How do you usually **communicate** with your friends and family?

2. What is one thing that you do on a **normal** day?

BRAINSTORMING

C List things that you think most people around the world do every day. Share your ideas with a partner.

brush teeth

daily activities

SCANNING/
PREDICTING

D Scan for the numbers in the first paragraph. Then look at the words around them. What do you think the passage is about? Check your answer as you read.

a. a day in the life of a movie director

b a very unusual day on our planet

c. a movie about one day on Earth

A DAY ON PLANET EARTH

🎧 1

What happens in a single day on planet Earth? In 2010, a **team** led by film director Kevin Macdonald tried to find out. The team asked people around the world to film their life on a single day—July 24—and to send in their videos.

A As a result, people **uploaded** 80,000 videos to YouTube—a total of more than 4,500 hours. The videos were sent by people from 192 countries, from Australia to Zambia. Macdonald's team used the videos to **produce** a 90-minute movie called *Life in a Day*.

The movie begins as most days begin. People wake up, get dressed, wash their faces, and brush their teeth. Parents **take care of** their children. People laugh

B and cry. As the day goes on, we see changes in people's lives. A man thanks the hospital workers who helped save his life. A woman learns that she is pregnant.[1] A man calls his mother and asks, "What should I say to the woman I love?"

[1] If a woman or a female animal is **pregnant**, she is going to have a baby or babies.

▲ **Skydiver Vania Da Rui was one of thousands of contributors to the *Life in a Day* project.**

C   Macdonald understood that what may be **normal** to one person may be **extraordinary** to another. For example, the movie shows cultural differences in the different ways that people travel to work. Macdonald explains, "What we might see as banal, living in our own culture, is not banal to somebody growing up in Dakar."[2]

D   Macdonald's team also asked people the following questions: "What do you love most in the world, and what do you fear?" People speak of their love for family and friends, of football and fast cars, a pet cat, or even a refrigerator. Children speak of being scared of imaginary monsters[3] and of real-life lions. Some Ukrainian farmers worry that wolves are going to eat their goats. People around the world talk about their fear of guns, of war, and of the loss of natural beauty.

E   Macdonald says that *Life in a Day* was possible because of the way we are all **connected**. "The film is doing something that [was not] possible pre-Internet … The idea that you can ask thousands, tens of thousands, maybe hundreds of thousands of people all to contribute to a **project** and all to **communicate** about it and learn about it at the same time."

F   One of the people in the movie is a Korean cyclist named Okhwan Yoon. After traveling alone for nine years through 190 countries, he **arrived** on July 24 in Kathmandu, Nepal. "When I close my eyes," he says, "I can see all the different people in the world, from town to town, from country to country. I can feel it. I can touch it. I can see it." The *Life in a Day* team hopes that, after watching the movie, others may feel the same way.

▼ **Round-the-world cyclist Okhwan Yoon at the movie screening of *Life in a Day***

[2] **Dakar** is the capital city of Senegal in West Africa.
[3] **Monsters** are creatures in stories that are ugly and scary.

UNDERSTANDING THE READING

A What was the main purpose of the *Life in a Day* project?

UNDERSTANDING
MAIN IDEAS

    a. to describe a day of adventure for certain people around the world

    b. to find out what an ideal day is like for people around the world

    c. to discover what people around the world do on an average day

B Circle the correct answers to complete the sentences.

UNDERSTANDING
DETAILS

  1. The scenes in *Life in a Day* were filmed by _____.

    a. a movie director   b. regular people

  2. The movie used scenes of people traveling to work to show that _____.

    a. what seems normal to some people could be interesting to other people

    b. the way people travel has changed a lot in the last 50 years

  3. According to the director, the Internet was important for his film because _____.

    a. it allowed a lot of people to be part of the creative process

    b. it helped the film become successful quickly

  4. The filmmakers hope that people watching the movie will feel _____.

    a. they can help people in other parts of the world

    b. connected to many other people around the world

CRITICAL THINKING   Use the **context**—the words around a word—to guess the meaning of a new word. The context can also help you decide the word's part of speech (noun, verb, adjective, etc.). For example: *The team asked people around the world to film their life on a <u>single</u> day—July 24—and to send in their videos.* We can guess from the context ("July 24") that *single* is an adjective that means "one."

C Find and underline the following words in the reading. Use the context to identify their meanings. Then match each word or phrase to its definition (1–4).

CRITICAL THINKING:
INFERRING MEANING

goes on (paragraph B)   **imaginary** (paragraph D)

banal (paragraph C)   **contribute** (paragraph E)

  1. _____ (v) continues; doesn't stop

  2. _____ (adj) not real; made-up; fictional

  3. _____ (adj) boring; not interesting or unusual

  4. _____ (v) to give something for a particular purpose

D Imagine you are making a video to send to a life-in-a-day project. What part of your daily life would you film? Share your ideas with a partner.

CRITICAL THINKING:
APPLYING

I would send a video of _____

because _____.

DEVELOPING READING SKILLS

> ### READING SKILL Skimming for Gist
>
> When you skim for gist, you look at a passage quickly to find out what it basically means. You don't need to read every word. As you skim, pay attention to key phrases and words such as repeated nouns. You should also look for clues found in titles, photos, and subtitles to help you understand the overall topic. Knowing the gist of a passage can help you predict the kind of information you will learn from it.

SKIMMING FOR GIST

A Skim the paragraph below quickly. Pay attention to the key words higlighted. What is it about? Circle the topic (a–c). Then read the paragraph again slowly and check your answer.

   a. how long a day is on different planets

   b. how far the Earth moves in 24 hours

   c. how long it takes to travel to Jupiter

We all know that a single day is 24 hours long. However, that is only true for a day on planet Earth. That's because it takes the Earth 24 hours to make one rotation, or turn. Different planets take different amounts of time to rotate. So how long is one day on some of the other planets in our solar system? One day on the planet Mercury takes over 58 days in Earth time. That's a long day, but Venus has the longest day. A day on the planet Venus is 243 Earth days long. Jupiter, the largest planet, has the shortest day—just 9.9 Earth hours.

SKIMMING FOR GIST

B Skim the paragraph below quickly and circle the topic (a–c). Then read the paragraph again slowly and check your answer.

   a. ideas for a child's birthday

   b. why people need a lot of sleep

   c. a typical day after you have a baby

Are you about to have your first baby? Are you wondering what your typical day will be like? Well, it will definitely be very different from your typical day now. First, you won't sleep for 8 hours at night and stay awake for the other 16 hours of the day. You will probably sleep when your baby sleeps and be awake when your baby is awake. Babies have different sleep patterns, but your baby will probably sleep for 1 to 3 hours at a time. When you are awake, you will probably spend a lot of your time feeding your baby and changing diapers. Expect to be tired most of the time. But you can also expect to feel incredible happiness when you look at your beautiful new baby.

Video

A GLOBAL CONVERSATION

A group of teenagers take part in a Skype conversation as part of a project called "Do Remember Me."

BEFORE VIEWING

A Look at the photo and read the title and caption. Who do you think the people are talking to?

PREDICTING

B Read the information below and answer the questions. Then discuss with a partner.

LEARNING ABOUT THE TOPIC

Artist Sannii Crespina-Flores meets with American teens in Philadelphia twice a week. She gets them to talk to other teens from around the world through Skype. They are part of a project called "Do Remember Me." The goal of the project is to connect individuals and their communities, and build global relationships. The teens talk with young people from Kazakhstan, France, and Nigeria, and ask each other questions about their lives.

1. How do you think this project can help build global relationships?

_____

2. Why do you think they communicate through Skype?

_____

3. What kinds of questions do you think the teens ask each other?

_____

C The words in **bold** below are used in the video. Read the sentences. Then match each word to its definition.

> Magicians often **amaze** people through their performances.
>
> In the meeting, there was an **exchange** of ideas between the two leaders.
>
> My brother and I look so **alike** that people often think we are twins.

1. _____ (adj) similar

2. _____ (v) to make someone feel surprised

3. _____ (n) the giving and receiving of something

WHILE VIEWING

A ▶ Watch the video. Circle the correct answers.

1. The participants of the project share information about
   their country's history / their daily lives.

2. Besides talking to each other online, the teens share their experiences by
   visiting the other countries / recording videos of themselves.

3. Crespina-Flores thinks that through this project, the teens will see
   that people are more similar than different / the importance of teamwork.

B ▶ Watch the video again. Match the groups of teens to what they share as part of the project.

_____ 1. Female teens in the U.S.   a. perform a dance.

_____ 2. Teens in Kazakhstan   b. does a beatbox performance.

_____ 3. A teen in France   c. have a snowball fight.

_____ 4. Male teens in the U.S.   d. show a day in the fall.

AFTER VIEWING

A Discuss these questions with a partner.

1. At the end of the video, one teen says, "The world is as big or as small as you make it." What does this mean? Explain it in your own words.

2. If you could Skype people your age in other countries, what questions would you ask?

_____

_____

B What does the movie *Life in a Day* have in common with Sannii Crespina-Flores's Skype project? Share your ideas with a partner.

Reading 2

PREPARING TO READ

BUILDING VOCABULARY

A The words in **blue** below are used in the reading passage on pages 12–13. Complete each sentence with the correct form of the word or phrase.

balance	depend on	during	realize
spend time	schedule	surprise	measure

1. An employee's paycheck sometimes _____ their work hours. When the employee works more hours, they get a bigger paycheck.

2. It's important to _____ your work and your personal life. Make sure you're able to _____ with your family and friends when you aren't working.

3. Some people sleep _____ the day and work at night.

4. My family gave me a big _____ .They had planned a secret party on my birthday.

5. Everyone makes mistakes, but it's important that you _____ your mistakes and learn from them.

6. Nowadays, it's easy to check the _____ of trains and buses through an app.

7. We use a weighing scale to _____ how heavy something is.

USING VOCABULARY

B Discuss these questions with a partner.

1. What kinds of things do you do for fun **during** your free time?

2. What do you **spend** the most **time** doing in your free time? Why?

BRAINSTORMING

C Note your answers to the questions below. Then share your ideas with a partner.

1. What are some jobs that you think are interesting? Why?

_____

2. What is your dream job?

_____

PREDICTING

D Look at the photos and captions in the reading passage on pages 12–13. Match the people to what you think they do. Then check your answers as you read the passage.

_____ 1. Kakani Katija   a. takes images and films of people and places

_____ 2. Christine Lee   b. explores the lives of people in the past

_____ 3. Ricky Qi   c. studies marine animals

A DAY IN A LIFE

What is it like to be a National Geographic Explorer?
Three explorers describe their working lives.

Name: Ricky Qi
Job: Filmmaker and photographer

🎧 2

Ricky Qi takes images and videos to tell stories about people and places.

What time do you normally start and end your workday?
That depends on the part of the project I'm working on. Before and after filming, I usually wake up at 7 a.m., start working soon after that, and stop in the afternoon. During filming, I don't have a regular schedule. I usually wake up when the sun comes up and I quit when the sun goes down.

Where do you work?
That also depends on the project. I work from home when I'm not filming. While I'm filming, I work all over the world. For example, when I was making a film about the Himalayas, I worked in a village in the mountains.

Why did you choose to do this kind of work?
When I was young, I watched a lot of movies and read a lot of books. They showed me different ways of living and thinking. I want my films and photographs to do this for other people!

What's the most difficult thing about your job?
The paperwork. It's boring, but it's important.

Kakani Katija studies the movements of jellyfish and other ocean animals.

Name: Kakani Katija
Job: Bioengineer

Where do you work?
Sometimes I work in my office or with animals in a laboratory. I **spend** a lot of **time** in the ocean, too. I dive with animals to learn how they swim and eat.

What time do you normally start and end your workday?
I often keep a nine-to-five schedule. When I am studying animals in the ocean, my start and end times depend on the behavior of the animals.

What's the most difficult thing about your job?
It's tough to **balance** my work schedule, travel, and time with my family.

What's one of the strangest things that happened to you at work?
One night I was diving in Woods Hole, Massachusetts. I was **measuring** a jellyfish. Suddenly, a crab swam up. It grabbed the jellyfish in its claws and ate him! It was a big **surprise**!

Christine Lee studies the skeletons of ancient humans to understand how they lived.

Name: Christine Lee
Job: Bioarchaeologist

Where do you work?
I work on archaeological excavations[1] in China and Mongolia. I also work in a professor's office and in a laboratory.

What time do you normally start and end your workday?
If I am on an archaeological excavation, I usually work from sunrise to sundown. In the laboratory, I work as long as the laboratory is open.

What's the best thing about your job?
Finding a story that has been buried for hundreds or thousands of years.

What's the toughest thing about your job?
Cold weather, no bathrooms!

What's one of the strangest things that happened to you at work?
When I was working on two children's skeletons, the skulls started moving back and forth. Luckily, I **realized** there was a rainstorm coming. The wind was moving the skulls!

[1]In an **archaeological excavation**, scientists look for things buried in the ground to learn about the past.

UNDERSTANDING THE READING

UNDERSTANDING PURPOSE

A What is the purpose of the passage?

a. to show a single day in the lives of three National Geographic Explorers

b. to show what daily life is like for three National Geographic Explorers

c. to show how three National Geographic Explorers worked together on one day

UNDERSTANDING DETAILS

B Complete the Venn diagram using the descriptions (a–h).

a. examines bones

b. works in a lab sometimes

c. often dives in the ocean

d. doesn't like paperwork

e. has an irregular schedule

f. was inspired by movies and books

g. talks about a strange thing that happened

h. finds it difficult to balance work and personal time

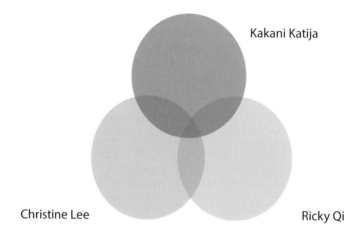

Kakani Katija

Christine Lee

Ricky Qi

CRITICAL THINKING: INFERRING MEANING

C Find and underline these words on pages 12–13. Use context to identify their meanings. Then match each word to its definition.

| laboratory | dive | skeleton | buried | quit |

1. _____ (v) to stop

2. _____ (adj) covered up; hidden

3. _____ (n) all the bones in a person's or an animal's body

4. _____ (v) to go down under the surface of a sea or lake

5. _____ (n) a room or building where scientific work is done

CRITICAL THINKING: REFLECTING

D What do you think was most interesting about each person's job? Make notes below.

Kakani Katija: _____

Christine Lee: _____

Ricky Qi: _____

Share your ideas with a partner. Who do you think has the most interesting job?

Writing

EXPLORING WRITTEN ENGLISH

A Read the sentences below. Write **R** if the sentence describes a routine. Write **GF** if it describes a general fact.

NOTICING

1. Kakani Katija and Christine Lee are scientists. _____
2. The world's population is about 7 billion people. _____
3. My family watches movies every weekend. _____
4. I don't go to the office on the weekends. _____
5. Kevin Macdonald is the director of *Life in a Day*. _____

LANGUAGE FOR WRITING Simple Present Tense

Use the simple present for habits and daily routines.

*Sometimes I **work** in my office.*
*I **don't have** classes on Tuesdays.*
*Every day, more than eight million people **travel** by plane.*

Also use the simple present for facts or general statements about people and places:

*A single day **is** 24 hours long.*
*Christine Lee **studies** the skeletons of ancient humans.*
*It **takes** the Earth 24 hours to make one rotation.*
*In northern Finland the sun **doesn't set** in the summer.*

Note: To create the negative form, add *doesn't* or *don't* to the base verb.

B Complete each sentence (1–6) with the correct simple present form of a verb from the box below. Some words can be used twice.

be	communicate	have	leave	do	take	work

Example: Every day, I _____leave_____ my house at 7:00 a.m.

1. I often _____ with my friends by email.

2. We _____ all connected through the Internet.

3. A day on Jupiter _____ less than 10 Earth hours long.

4. She only _____ Mondays to Fridays. She _____ not _____ on weekends.

5. I _____ two cats. My neighbor also _____ two cats.

6. I _____ the train to work every morning.

C Write complete sentences to answer the questions below.

Example: What is your name?

My name is John.

Where do you live?

I live in Los Angeles.

1. What is your favorite hobby?

   _____

2. Where do you like to go for vacations?

   _____

3. What is your favorite movie?

   _____

4. What do you usually do on weekends?

   _____

5. How do you get to class every day?

   _____

6. Where do you study?

   _____

7. What does your family enjoy doing?

   _____

WRITING SKILL Writing Good Sentences

These three tips will help you write good sentences:

1. Make sure every sentence has a subject and at least one verb.

   I often **keep** a nine-to-five schedule.

2. Combine simple ideas to avoid short sentences.

   Sometimes I work in my office. Sometimes I work with animals. I work with them in a laboratory.

   → *Sometimes I work in my office, but sometimes I work with animals in a laboratory.*

3. Check that you are using the correct form of a verb for each subject.

   *Different planets **take** different amounts of time to rotate.*
   *One day on the planet Mercury **takes** over 58 days in Earth time.*

D Edit each sentence or set of sentences using the tips in the Writing Skill box.

Example: I studies English on Mondays, Wednesdays, and Fridays.

I study English on Mondays, Wednesdays, and Fridays.

1. I work in an office. It is on First Street.

   _____

2. My friend and I like to plays computer games.

   _____

3. My best friend's name John.

   _____

4. I like the movie *Iron Man*. It's my favorite movie.

   _____

5. My family likes to go hiking. We hike in the mountains. We hike in the summer.

   _____

6. We eats dinner at 7:00 every evening.

   _____

7. One of my favorite sports are basketball.

   _____

E Write three sentences about your favorite weekend activities.

1. _____

2. _____

3. _____

F Work with two other classmates. Ask them about their favorite weekend activities and make notes below. How similar or different are they from your favorite activities?

Student 1: _____

_____

_____

Student 2: _____

_____

_____

WRITING TASK

> **GOAL** You are going to write sentences on the following topic:
> Describe three of your daily activities that might be interesting to someone from another country.

BRAINSTORMING **A** Brainstorm a list of things that you do in a typical day.

Things I do in a typical day

PLANNING **B** Follow these steps to make notes for your sentences. Don't worry about grammar or spelling. Don't write complete sentences.

Step 1 Look at your brainstorming notes from exercise A. Choose three activities that you think someone from another country might find interesting.

Step 2 Decide how you want to organize your ideas. For example, you could put the activities in the order that you do them every day. You could also put the most interesting activity at the end.

Step 3 Include at least one detail for each activity.

Things I Do in a Typical Day	Details (when, why, who with, etc.)
take a boat across the lake	every morning at 8 fastest way to get to my office
1.	
2.	
3.	

FIRST DRAFT **C** Use the information in your outline to write a first draft of your sentences.

REVISING PRACTICE

The drafts below are similar to the one you are going to write, but they are on a different topic:

Describe three leisure activities. Give one or more details about each one. For example, explain when, why, or where you do them or who you do them with.

What did the writer do in Draft 2 to improve the sentences? Match the changes (a–d) to the highlighted parts. Some can be used more than once.

a. replaced an unrelated idea with a new one
b. added a detail about an idea
c. corrected a verb form
d. combined two short sentences

Draft 1

I usually do my homework on Saturday morning.

My friends and I usually go to the movies. We go on Saturdays.

I practice the guitar every day after school. Sometimes my friends comes over and we play the guitar together.

Draft 2

I play tennis in the park on Sunday mornings. It's fun and it's ☐ ☐

good exercise.

My friends and I usually go to the movies on Saturdays. ☐

We go to the movie theater in the mall. ☐

I practice the guitar every day after school. Sometimes my friends ☐

come over and we play the guitar together.

D   **Now use the questions below to revise your sentences.**   REVISED DRAFT

  ☐ Are all your sentences about daily activities?

  ☐ Did you include at least one detail for each activity?

  ☐ Are all the verb forms correct?

  ☐ Did you combine short sentences where suitable?

EDITING PRACTICE

Read the information below.

In sentences using the simple present tense, remember to:
- use the correct form of be: am, is, or are.
- use the correct form of other verbs (e.g., go/goes, eat/eats, talk/talks).
- use the correct form of do and the base form of a verb in negative statements (e.g., don't take / doesn't take).

Correct one mistake with the simple present tense in each of the sentences (1–8).

1. I cooks food for 500 people every day.

2. I think many people doesn't cook nowadays.

3. My husband drive me to work every morning.

4. He be a bus driver.

5. I don't works in an office.

6. I working in a laboratory.

7. My grandparents doesn't watch TV.

8. My daughter doesn't has a job.

FINAL DRAFT **E** Follow these steps to write a final draft.

1. Check your revised draft for mistakes with simple present verb forms.

2. Now use the checklist on page 218 to write a final draft. Make any other necessary changes.

UNIT REVIEW

Answer the following questions.

1. Whose daily life in this unit would you like to know more about? What would you like to know?

_____

_____

_____

2. What clues can help you find the main idea of a passage?

_____

_____

_____

3. Do you remember the meanings of these words? Check (✓) the ones you know. Look back at the unit and review the ones you don't know.

Reading 1:

☐ arrive   ☐ communicate AWL   ☐ connect
☐ extraordinary   ☐ normal AWL   ☐ produce
☐ project AWL   ☐ take care of   ☐ team AWL
☐ upload

Reading 2:

☐ balance   ☐ depend on   ☐ during
☐ measure   ☐ realize   ☐ schedule AWL
☐ spend time   ☐ surprise

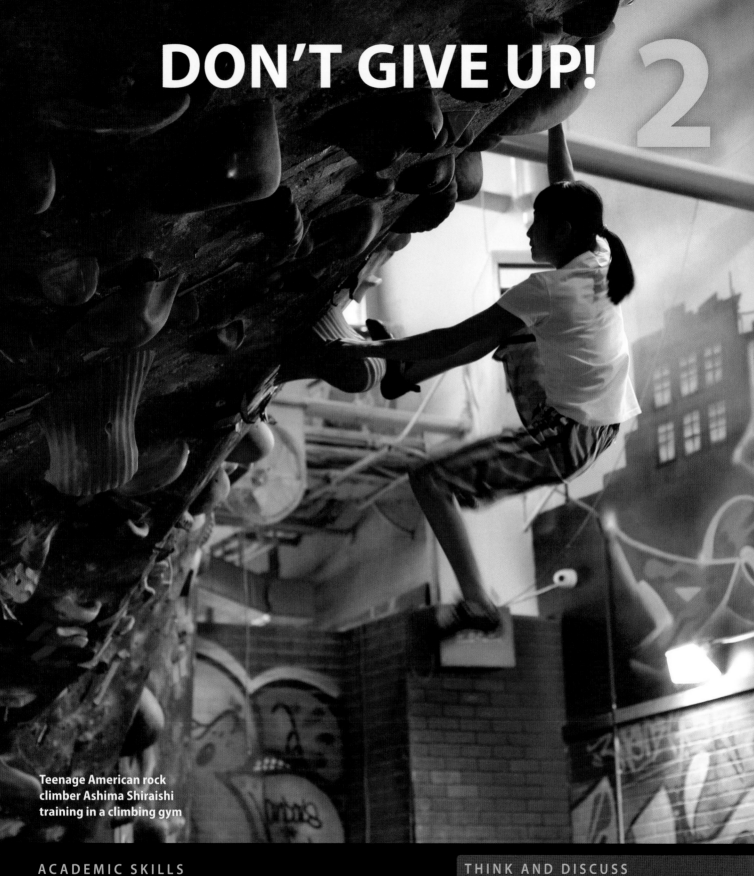

DON'T GIVE UP! 2

Teenage American rock climber Ashima Shiraishi training in a climbing gym

ACADEMIC SKILLS

READING Identifying main ideas of paragraphs
WRITING Ordering ideas
GRAMMAR Using *want* and *need*
CRITICAL THINKING Identifying evidence

THINK AND DISCUSS

1 What kind of challenges do you think young people face when they study at school?
2 How does school prepare you for life?

A Look at the information on these pages and answer the questions.

1. Where in the world are literacy rates high? Where are they low?

2. In which parts of the world do many children go to school? In which parts do many children *not* go to school?

3. What is one reason some children don't go to school?

B Match the correct form of the words in **blue** to their definitions.

_____ (v) to be present at

_____ (adj) the early years of school

_____ (n) learning or training in schools

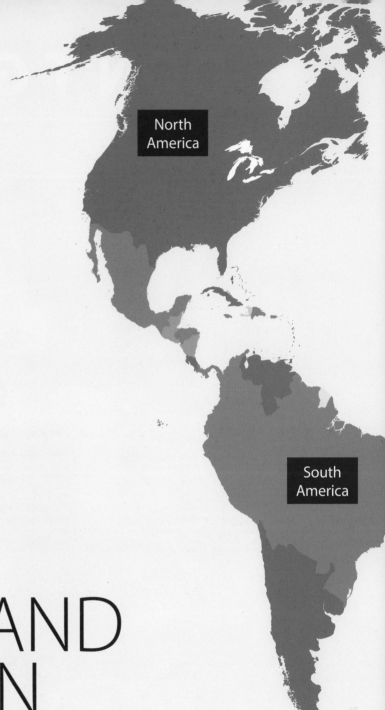

North America

South America

LITERACY AND EDUCATION

About 800 million adults around the world are illiterate; that is, they cannot read and write.[1] Ninety percent of these people live in poor countries, and two-thirds of them are women. Illiteracy is especially common in poor countries because many families are not able to pay for their children's **education**. In fact, about 60 million young children worldwide do not go to **primary** school, and about 70 million older children do not **attend** secondary school. This makes it more difficult for them to get good jobs and increase their standard of living.

[1]Source: United Nations Educational, Scientific and Cultural Organization

Literacy rate
Percent of total population
age 15 and over, 2013

- 95% – 100%
- 85% – 94.9%
- 75% – 84.9%
- 65% – 74.9%
- Less than 65%
- No data available

Percent of primary school-age
children not in school
Latest available data

- More than 16.0%
- 8.0% – 16.0%
- 3.9% – 7.9%
- 1.4% – 3.8%
- Less than 1.4%
- No data available

Reading 1

PREPARING TO READ

BUILDING
VOCABULARY

A The words in **blue** below are used in the reading passage on pages 25–26. Read the paragraph. Then match the correct form of each word to its definition.

There are several reasons why many children around the world do not attend school. One reason is that the **governments** of many poor countries do not have money to provide good school facilities or train teachers. Schools in poor countries often do not have things that people in richer countries may think are **ordinary** or basic, such as classrooms or bathrooms. Also, in some cultures, people **believe** that education is more important for boys than for girls. As a result, families often **decide** to keep their daughters at home.

1. _____ (adj) normal, and not special in any way

2. _____ (v) to think something is true

3. _____ (v) to choose something after thinking about it

4. _____ (n) the group of people who control and organize a country

BUILDING
VOCABULARY

B Read the sentences. Choose the best definitions for the words in **blue**.

1. **Motivated** students usually enjoy school and are excited about learning.

   a. having an interest in doing something   b. having high intelligence

2. Students who are **independent** don't need teachers or parents to tell them to do their homework.

   a. wanting people to like them   b. not needing help from other people

3. School **leaders** often help the teacher organize the class and take care of other students.

   a. people who guide other people   b. people who follow orders

USING
VOCABULARY

C Discuss these questions with a partner.

1. What **primary** school did you **attend**? Describe it.

2. Which school subject makes/made you feel the most **motivated**? Why?

BRAINSTORMING

D List three useful things you learned in primary school. Share your list with your partner.

_____

PREDICTING

E Look at the photo and read the title of the reading passage on page 25. Why do you think the man is studying in a class with children? Discuss with a partner. Then check your ideas as you read the passage.

THE WORLD'S OLDEST FIRST GRADER

🎧 3

A   On January 12, 2004, Kimani Maruge knocked on the door of the primary school in his village in Kenya. It was the first day of school, and he was ready to start learning. The teacher let him in and gave him a desk. The new student sat down with the rest of the first graders: six- and seven-year-old children. However, Kimani Maruge was not an ordinary first grader. He was 84 years old—the world's oldest first grader.

FIGHTING TO STAY IN SCHOOL

B   Kimani Maruge was born in Kenya in 1920. At that time, primary education in Kenya was not free, and Maruge's family didn't have enough money to pay for school. When Maruge grew up, he worked hard as a farmer. In the 1950s, he fought with other Kenyans against the British colonists.[1] After years of fighting, Kenya became independent in 1963.

C   In 2003, the Kenyan government began offering free primary education to everyone, and Maruge wanted an education, too. However, it wasn't always easy for him to attend school. Many of the first graders' parents didn't want an old man in their children's class. School officials[2] said that a primary education was only for children. But the school principal,[3] Jane Obinchu, believed Maruge was right. With her help, he was able to stay in school.

[1] colonists: people who live in a foreign country that is controlled by their country
[2] official: a person who has an important position in an organization, such as a government or a school
[3] principal: the person in charge of a school

Maruge and his schoolmates at a school parade

D   Maruge was a **motivated** and successful student. While in primary school, he studied Swahili,[4] English, and math. He did well in these subjects. In fact, he was one of the top five students in his first grade class. By the second grade, Maruge became the school's student **leader**. And even though life was sometimes difficult, Maruge stayed in school until the seventh grade.

E   In 2008, Maruge had to move to a refugee camp because of fighting in his village. However, even during those difficult times he continued to go to school. Later that year, he moved to a home for the elderly. Some of the residents of the home were illiterate, and Maruge taught them to read and write. He also continued going to school.

INSPIRED[5] TO LEARN

F   In 2005, Maruge flew in a plane for the first time in his life. He traveled to New York City, where he gave a speech at the United Nations. He spoke about the importance of education and asked for help to educate the people of Kenya. Maruge also wanted to improve primary education for children in Africa.

G   Maruge died in 2009 at age 89, but his story continues to inspire many people. The 2010 movie *The First Grader* showed Maruge's amazing fight to get an education. After watching the movie, many older Kenyans **decided** to start school. One of those people was 19-year-old Thoma Litei. Litei said, "I knew it was not too late. I wanted to read, and to know more language, so I came [to school] to learn. That is why it is important for his story to be known."

[4]**Swahili:** a language spoken in much of East Africa
[5]**inspire:** to give you new ideas or make you want to do something

UNDERSTANDING THE READING

A Choose the correct option to complete the sentence about the reading passage.

UNDERSTANDING MAIN IDEAS

The World's Oldest First Grader is about an old man who _____ .

a. fought a war so he could attend primary school
b. became a film actor after studying at school
c. faced many difficulties to attend primary school

B Use the words in the box to complete the phrases about events in Maruge's life.

UNDERSTANDING DETAILS

> movie   farmer   refugee camp   principal   taught   spoke   war

a. started work as a _____
b. a _____ about his life was made
c. fought in a _____ against the British
d. _____ elderly people to read and write
e. got help from a _____ to go to primary school
f. went to New York and _____ at the United Nations
g. moved to a _____ and continued going to school

C Complete the timeline with the events in exercise B.

SEQUENCING

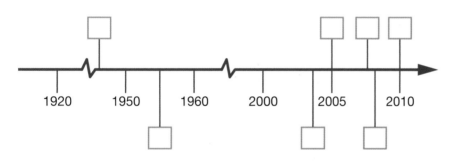

1920   1950   1960   2000   2005   2010

> **CRITICAL THINKING**   When you read a text, look closely to **identify evidence** that supports your ideas, or assumptions, about it.

D How would you describe Maruge's character? Write three adjectives, and find information from the passage to support each one. Then share your ideas with a partner.

CRITICAL THINKING: IDENTIFYING EVIDENCE

Adjectives   Reasons

1. _____   _____

2. _____   _____

3. _____   _____

DEVELOPING READING SKILLS

The main idea of a paragraph is the idea that the paragraph focuses on. A good paragraph usually has one main idea. Other ideas in the paragraph support the main idea by describing or explaining it. The main idea is usually—but not always—given at the beginning or the end of the paragraph.

IDENTIFYING
MAIN IDEAS

A Read the paragraph below. Then answer questions 2 and 3.

As a child, Kakenya Ntaiya was like most other girls in her village in Kenya. By the time she was a teenager, she was expected to marry and have children. Instead, Ntaiya convinced her parents to let her finish high school. After that, she went to the United States to attend college. She eventually got a PhD in education. When Ntaiya returned home in 2009, she started the Kakenya Center for Excellence boarding school. Now almost 280 girls in her little village are getting a primary school education. Education changed Ntaiya's life, so she hopes her experience will inspire other girls to achieve their own life goals.

1. Topic of the paragraph: *Kakenya Ntaiya*

2. What is the main idea of the paragraph?

   a. Kenyan girls often do not get an education because they must marry at a young age.
   b. Through her hard work, a Kenyan woman went to college in the United States.
   c. A Kenyan woman got an education and is now helping Kenyan girls improve their lives.

3. Which sentence in the paragraph summarizes the main idea?

   a. the first sentence   b. the third sentence   c. the last sentence

IDENTIFYING
MAIN IDEAS

B Look back at the reading passage on pages 25–26. Match each main idea below to one of these paragraphs from the passage: **A, C, E,** or **G.**

_____ 1. Maruge was an inspiration to other adult Kenyans.

_____ 2. Maruge faced many challenges when he started school.

_____ 3. Maruge was unlike ordinary first graders.

_____ 4. Maruge did not stop studying, even when it was difficult.

▶ **Kakenya Ntaiya reads with students at her school.**

Video

A SCHOOL FOR CHANGE

At SOLA, students live in the school, and study a wide range of subjects.

BEFORE VIEWING

A Look at the photo, the caption, and the title of the video. What do you think is special about this school? Discuss your ideas with a partner.

PREDICTING

B Read the information about Afghanistan. Then answer the questions.

LEARNING ABOUT THE TOPIC

Afghanistan has seen great improvements in education. But it is still difficult for girls and women there to get an education. One reason is tradition—some families believe girls don't need to go to school. Many families also don't have money to send their children to school. Violence is another problem—it's often not safe for girls to attend school. As a result, only 12 percent of Afghan women are literate, and 38 percent of children (the majority of them girls) are not able to go to school.

1. What are three reasons that it is still difficult for Afghan girls to go to school?

_____

2. Which diagram below shows the school attendance among Afghan children?

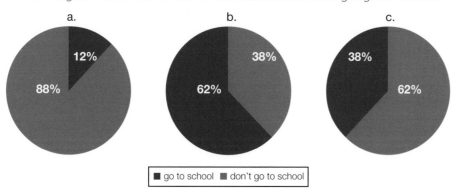

a.	b.	c.
12% / 88%	38% / 62%	38% / 62%

■ go to school ■ don't go to school

C The words in **bold** below are used in the video. Read the paragraph. Then match the correct form of each word to its definition.

Many families in Afghanistan don't think getting an education is the number one **priority** for their daughters, so only a **minority** of women in Afghanistan can read and write. In poor families, older children may have to take care of their **siblings** instead of going to school.

1. _____ (n) a brother or sister

2. _____ (n) a number or group that is less than half of the total

3. _____ (n) something that has greater importance than something else

WHILE VIEWING

A ▶ Watch the video. What are some benefits of girls attending this school? Check (✓) the items mentioned.

They can _____.

☐ 1. get a good job   ☐ 4. become global citizens

☐ 2. experience other countries' cultures   ☐ 5. get into a college overseas

☐ 3. help their country   ☐ 6. become leaders of their country

B ▶ Watch the video again. Circle T for *true* or F for *false*.

1. Basij-Rasikh's parents believed education wasn't important for girls.   T   F

2. Basij-Rasikh had no opportunity to go to school.   T   F

3. The students at SOLA feel positive about their future.   T   F

4. Basij-Rasikh believes that problems in Afghanistan should be solved by its own people.   T   F

AFTER VIEWING

A Discuss these questions with a partner.

1. The school aims to teach students to be global citizens. What do you think being a global citizen means?
2. In what two ways is Basij-Rasikh similar to Kimani Maruge?

B Work with a partner. Basij-Rasikh states that educating a girl benefits her family, her community, and our world. Can you think of examples of what she means?

How does educating a girl benefit …?

her family: _____

her community: _____

the world: _____

Reading 2

PREPARING TO READ

BUILDING VOCABULARY

A The words in blue below are used in the reading passage on pages 32–33. Read the paragraph. Then match the correct form of each word or phrase to its definition.

There are a few ways you can learn new words and improve your vocabulary **skills**. One way is to look up the meaning of words in a dictionary, then **record** them in a notebook. If there are words with **similar** meanings, such as *small* and *tiny*, grouping them together can make them easier to remember. It may be difficult at first to remember so many new words, but it's important to keep practicing and not **give up**!

1. _____ (n) an ability

2. _____ (adj) almost the same

3. _____ (v) to stop doing something halfway

4. _____ (v) to write or keep information for the future

BUILDING VOCABULARY

B Complete the sentences below with the correct form of the words in blue. Use a dictionary to help you.

solve	program	advice	develop

1. Schools have many different _____ that teach students different skills.

2. If you need help with choosing a college, you can ask a teacher for _____.

3. A lot of time and effort is needed to _____ the problem of illiteracy in poorer countries.

4. Private schools are usually allowed to _____ and design their own courses.

USING VOCABULARY

C Discuss these questions with a partner.

1. Do you know anyone who has any special **skills**?
2. How do you think they **developed** those skills?

PREDICTING

D Read the first paragraph of the reading passage on page 32. Think of some possible reasons for Duckworth's observation. Share your ideas with a partner. Then check your ideas as you read the passage.

They got help from their parents. _____

_____

_____

THE SECRET OF SUCCESS?

In the late 1990s, a New York City schoolteacher named Angela Duckworth made a surprising discovery. Some of the smartest kids in her math classes were getting the lowest grades, and some of the kids with lower IQ scores[1] were getting the highest. Why was this happening?

SOLVING THE PUZZLE

To try to solve this mystery, Duckworth entered a PhD program in psychology at the University of Pennsylvania. She began to research people in a variety of fields—salespeople, college students, army cadets,[2] and teachers in poor neighborhoods. She asked people to rate themselves using a list of statements—for example, "I finish whatever I begin." In another study, she recorded people's responses to questions such as, "Would you rather have a dollar now or two dollars tomorrow?"

From her research, Duckworth realized that many successful people—salespeople who made the most money, or teachers who improved their students' grades the most—have similar personality traits. First of all, they have self-control—the ability to avoid distractions[3] and get things done. A person with self-control has the patience to wait for something better to happen in the future.

In addition, Duckworth noticed that successful people have determination, or "grit." People with grit work hard and don't give up. They stay with a task even if it's hard, or if it takes a long time.

MAKING A DIFFERENCE

Is it possible to develop self-control and grit? Duckworth believes so. One way, she suggests, is to follow the "Hard Thing" rule: Choose a skill that is hard for you, such as learning a new language, or

An adventurer walking on a highline above Rio de Janeiro

playing a musical instrument. Practice it daily, even if you don't feel like it. Don't give up! To be successful, you need to stay with it. Duckworth also advises changing habits to avoid distractions. For example, put your phone away when you're studying. "Children know these tricks," she says, "but adults sometimes forget them."

F   To be successful at what you do, Duckworth has this **advice**: Decide on something you really want to achieve, and find people who will support you. You also need to practice, practice, practice. As she says in her book *Grit*, "… if you create a vision[4] for yourself and stick with it, you can make amazing things happen in your life."

[1]**IQ scores:** the results of a test that measures ability to understand and learn things
[2]**army cadets:** people who are training to become soldiers
[3]**distractions:** things that take your attention away from important tasks
[4]**vision:** an idea of the future

THE CHARACTERISTICS OF GRIT

Angela Duckworth studied successful people and found four basic characteristics of "gritty" people.
Interest: finding something they like and developing it
Practice: spending a lot of time doing something to become better at it
Purpose: feeling that what they're doing is important
Hope: having a positive attitude about the future

UNDERSTANDING THE READING

UNDERSTANDING PURPOSE

A Match each of these paragraphs from the passage to its purpose.

_____ 1. Paragraph A   a. to summarize what Duckworth discovered

_____ 2. Paragraph B   b. to show why Duckworth did her study

_____ 3. Paragraphs C–D   c. to explain how Duckworth tried to find an answer

_____ 4. Paragraphs E–F   d. to give advice to people who want to become more successful

SUMMARIZING

B Complete the summary of Duckworth's study in your own words.

Angela Duckworth found that successful people usually have two characteristics—grit and self-control. People with grit are able to _____

_____ , while people with self-control _____

_____ .

CATEGORIZING

C Read the quotes below. Which of them are examples of someone with grit, and which are of someone with self-control? Write G for *grit* and S for *self-control*.

_____ 1. "My friends asked me out to a concert today, but I said no because I need to study for a test tomorrow."

_____ 2. "I failed my driving test several times, but I managed to pass on the fifth time after practicing a lot."

_____ 3. "I wanted to go to art school, but my parents didn't like the idea. However, I spent time talking to them about my dream and they understood how important it was to me."

_____ 4. "I wanted to buy a new laptop, but I decided to save the money since my laptop is still working."

CRITICAL THINKING: INFERRING

D Which advice below would Duckworth probably give?

a. Only do the things that you like most.
b. Challenge yourself and don't give up halfway.
c. Start with an easy skill first before trying something harder.

CRITICAL THINKING: APPLYING

E Think of two people you know who have the characteristics Duckworth describes.

Who?	Characteristic	Example
my uncle	determination	started learning the violin at 50, took lessons, and practiced every day

Writing

EXPLORING WRITTEN ENGLISH

A Read the sentences below and check (✓) the sentences that … NOTICING

1. describe things people *would like* to do.

☐ a. Basij-Rasikh wants to improve the lives of Afghan women through education.

☐ b. Maruge's family didn't have enough money to pay for school.

☐ c. Maruge wanted to get an education even though he was already in his eighties.

2. describe things people *have to* do.

☐ d. To be successful, you need to stay with it.

☐ e. You also need to practice, practice, practice.

☐ f. To try to solve this mystery, Duckworth entered a PhD program in psychology.

LANGUAGE FOR WRITING Using *want* and *need*

Use *want* with an infinitive (*to* + base verb) to describe things you *would like* to do (i.e., you have a choice) and *need* with an infinitive to describe things you *have to* do (i.e., you don't have a choice):

Older Kenyans saw The First Grader, and now they <u>want to go</u> back to school.

want + infinitive

I <u>need to study</u> English so I can improve my grade.

need + infinitive

You can also use *want* and *need* with noun phrases:

The students want <u>new laptops</u>. The school needs <u>more money</u> to pay its teachers.

Note that *need* and *want* have different meanings. You use *need* to talk about things that you can't do without, and *want* for things you wish for. For example, maybe you *don't want to* study for a test, but you *need to* study in order to get a good grade.

Now look at the sentences in exercise A again. Underline the words or phrases that introduce things that people are interested in doing or have to do.

B Unscramble the sentences (1–5).

Example: a mystery / solve / wanted / about her math students / to / Duckworth

<u>Duckworth wanted to solve a mystery about her math students.</u>

1. to school / to / some older Kenyans / want / go

_____

2. this month / an exam / take / to / need / we

_____

3. Maruge / the principal / to / to school / go / wanted

_____

4. study / some people / need / to / in a quiet place

_____

5. English-speaking employees / want / many companies / hire / to

_____

C Circle *want* or *need* to complete each sentence.

Example: The school **wants** /(**needs**)more students or it will have to close.

1. You can't attend a good university with a low TOEFL score; you **want** / **need** to do well on the test.

2. Some people **want** / **need** to learn Spanish because it's a beautiful language.

3. You don't **want** / **need** to have a college degree to work in a hotel.

4. I **want** / **need** to learn more about animals because I'm interested in them.

D Think about things that you *want* to do in the next five years and things that you *need* to do. Complete the chart.

Things I *want* to do in the next five years	Things I *need* to do in the next five years
visit Mexico	find a job

Now compare your chart with a partner's. Ask and answer questions about the information.

A: *What do you want to do in the next five years?*
B: *I want to visit Mexico.*

A: *What do you need to do in the next five years?*
B: *I need to find a job.*

Now write two sentences using *want* + infinitive and two sentences using *need* + infinitive based on the information in your chart.

_____

_____

_____

_____

When you write about how you plan to achieve a goal, organize your ideas in a logical way. For example, you can organize reasons in order of importance or as steps in a process.

To show your steps clearly, you can use words and phrases such as *first/firstly, second/ secondly, next, then, finally,* and *lastly*.

Note: When you list a series of ideas, use the same form of these words. For example, you can say *first, second, third*, or *firstly, secondly, thirdly*, but not *first, secondly, third*.

> *I want to study in Spain. **First**, I need to learn Spanish. **Then** I need to look for programs for foreigners in Spain.*

> *I want to improve my cooking skills. To do that, **first**, I need to sign up for a cooking class. **Second**, I need to study how people cook by watching cooking videos online.*

E Look at the goal and the list of steps for achieving it below. Put the steps in order (1–5).

Goal: Submit a college application.

_____ a. Complete and submit your applications.

_____ b. Decide what you want to study.

_____ c. Do online research; identify some colleges that have the courses you want.

_____ d. After learning more about your choices, decide on the colleges you want to apply to.

_____ e. Find out as much as you can about the colleges you're interested in, such as the school environment or school fees.

F Imagine you want to apply to a college. Use the information in exercise E to write the steps you need to take. Use the words in the Writing Skill box to help you.

I want to submit a college application. First, _____

_____

_____

_____

_____

_____

_____

WRITING TASK

> **GOAL** You are going to write sentences on the following topic:
> Describe a learning goal and explain what you need to do to achieve it.

BRAINSTORMING **A** Think about your learning goals. Note two ideas and then share them with a partner.

Things I want to learn (e.g., a subject, a language, a skill)	Places I can learn in (e.g., a country, a school, a training program)	Things I need to do/get (e.g., a degree, a certificate, a diploma)

PLANNING **B** Follow these steps to make notes for your sentences. Don't worry about grammar or spelling. Don't write complete sentences.

Step 1 Look at your brainstorming notes in exercise A. Choose one of your learning goals and write it in the outline below.

Step 2 List the three most important things you need to do in order to achieve your goal.

Step 3 Decide which things you need to do first and write them in order.

OUTLINE

My learning goal:

I want to _____

Things I need to do in order to achieve my goal:

I need to _____

_____

I need to _____

_____

I need to _____

_____

C Use the information in the outline to write a first draft of your sentences.

REVISING PRACTICE

The drafts below are similar to the one you are going to write, but they are on a different topic:

Describe a personal goal and explain what you need to do to achieve it.

What did the writer do in Draft 2 to improve the sentences? Match the changes (a–d) to the highlighted parts. Some can be used more than once.

a. stated the goal more clearly
b. organized ideas in a logical way
c. used a sequencing word or phrase
d. corrected a sentence with *want* or *need*

Draft 1

I want to buy a car.

Cars are expensive, so I need spend less money and save more.

I need to open a savings account at the bank and put money in it every month.

I need to make a budget and stick to it.

Lastly, to save money, I need to bring my lunch to work and not buy new clothes.

Draft 2

I want to buy a car so I can drive to my new job. ☐

Cars are expensive, so I need to spend less money and save more. ☐

First, I need to make a budget and stick to it. ☐ ☐

Next, I need to open a savings account at the bank and put money in it every month. ☐

Lastly, to save money, I need to bring my lunch to work and not buy new clothes.

D Now use the questions below to revise your sentences.

☐ Did you state your goal clearly?

☐ Did you organize your ideas in a logical way?

☐ Are all your actions related to your goal?

☐ Did you use *want* and *need* correctly?

EDITING PRACTICE

Read the information below.

In sentences using *want* or *need*, remember to:
- use an infinitive after *want* and *need*.
- use *want* if it is something you wish to do.
- use *need* if it is something you must do because you don't have a choice.

Correct one mistake with *want* or *need* in each of the sentences (1–5).

1. You need getting a passport before you can study in Canada.

2. Students want to take an entrance exam if they want to apply to college.

3. The school wants builds a new library next year.

4. Maruge went to primary school because he wanted learning to read.

5. I need writing an essay for my college application.

FINAL DRAFT   **E**   **Follow these steps to write a final draft.**

1. Check your revised draft for mistakes with *want* and *need* and ordering words.

2. Now use the checklist on page 218 to write a final draft. Make any other necessary changes.

UNIT REVIEW

Answer the following questions.

1. Which of Duckworth's advice do you think might be helpful for you?

_____

_____

_____

2. What are some words or phrases you can use to order a list of reasons or steps?

_____

_____

_____

3. Do you remember the meanings of these words? Check (✓) the ones you know. Look back at the unit and review the ones you don't know.

Reading 1:

☐ attend	☐ believe	☐ decide
☐ education	☐ government	☐ independent
☐ leader	☐ motivated **AWL**	☐ ordinary
☐ primary **AWL**		

Reading 2:

☐ advice	☐ develop	☐ give up
☐ program	☐ record	☐ similar **AWL**
☐ skill	☐ solve	

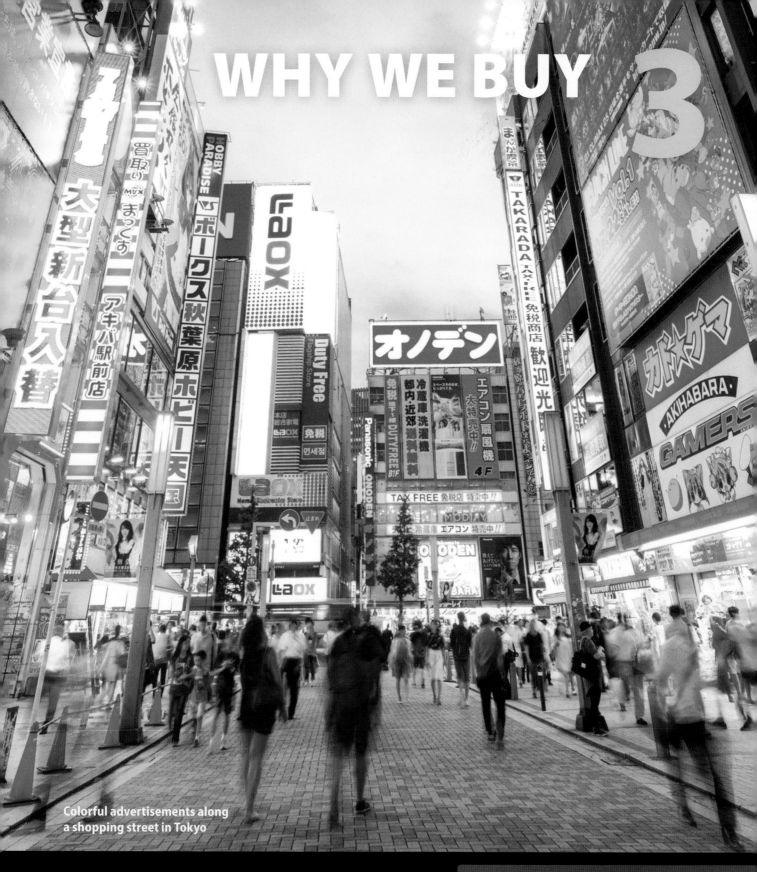

WHY WE BUY

3

Colorful advertisements along
a shopping street in Tokyo

ACADEMIC SKILLS

READING   Identifying supporting ideas

WRITING   Writing paragraphs and topic sentences

GRAMMAR   Connecting ideas

CRITICAL THINKING   Relating ideas

THINK AND DISCUSS

1   What kind of advertisements do you most
commonly see? Where do you see them?

2   How many advertisements do you think you
see in a day?

A Read the information on these pages and answer the questions.

1. What kind of advertising do most companies in the United States do?

2. What advertising method is more effective in getting people to spend money?

B Match the words in blue to their definitions.

_____ (n) one part of 100

_____ (n) something that is made for sale

_____ (v) to believe someone or something

A WORLD OF ADS

According to a 2014 study, a typical adult in the United States sees a few hundred advertisements—or ads—a day. These ads appear in a variety of ways: on posters, in magazines, on TV, and on the Internet. Among these, online advertising is the most popular way of reaching people. Companies in the United States are now spending more money on online ads than TV ads.

However, people seem to **trust** TV ads more than ads that they see on social media sites. A media organization in the United States reports that 37 **percent** of television viewers make buying decisions after watching TV ads, compared to 7 percent of people who buy a **product** after seeing ads on social media.

A huge ad covers the wall of a clothing store in Moscow.

Reading 1

PREPARING TO READ

BUILDING
VOCABULARY

A The words in **blue** below are used in the reading passage on pages 45–46. Read the paragraph. Then match the correct form of each word or phrase to its definition.

In 1994, Pizza Hut launched a website that allowed customers to order a pizza online **instead of** calling a restaurant. The first pizza ordered in this way was one of the first examples of online shopping. Since then, the number of online **stores** has grown quickly. Online shopping is an **attractive** option for many people: it allows them to shop at any time of the day and **avoid** crowds. In 2015, there were 1.46 billion online shoppers— about 20 percent of the world's population. And that figure continues to rise.

1. _____ (adj) nice, appealing

2. _____ (prep) in place of, as another option

3. _____ (n) a place where you can buy things

4. _____ (v) to stay away from something

BUILDING
VOCABULARY

B Read the sentences in the box. Then match the words in **blue** to their definitions.

> You can **control** the amount of money you spend by creating a savings plan.
>
> As society moves away from using **cash** and toward electronic payments, more people are comfortable with shopping online.
>
> Companies always need to improve their sales **strategies** in order to do better than their competitors.

When you …

1. **control** something, _____
2. pay in **cash**, _____
3. think of a **strategy**, _____

a. you give money in the form of coins and bills.
b. you make a plan for getting the best results.
c. you are able to do what you want with it.

USING
VOCABULARY

C Discuss these questions with a partner.

1. When do you usually pay in **cash**? When do you use other forms of payment?
2. What kinds of things do you buy online? What do you prefer to buy in a **store**? Why?

PREDICTING

D Work with a partner. Think about where you can find the following items in a supermarket: milk, fruit and vegetables, and candy. Why do you think supermarkets put these items in those places? Check your ideas as you read the passage.

WE LOVE FOOD™

THE PSYCHOLOGY OF SUPERMARKETS

△ Supermarkets are designed to make people spend more money.

🎧 5

A When we go shopping at a supermarket, we often buy more than we need. But it may not be our fault—supermarkets are controlling the way we shop. In fact, the whole experience of shopping for food is planned and arranged for us. Every detail of a supermarket has a purpose. The way the aisles are organized, the music, the lighting, the product advertising—all these things make us stay longer and spend more.

B From the moment we enter, a supermarket's floor plan controls the way we experience the store. There is usually only one way in and one way out, so we have to start and stop at particular places. Fruit and vegetables and the bakery are usually near the entrance. Fresh produce and the smell of bread baking can make a store seem fresh and attractive. This puts us in a good mood and makes us hungry, so we take our time and buy more food.

In addition, we often have to walk through the whole supermarket to find
what we need. For example, common items that most people shop for—like
milk and eggs—are usually at the back of the store. Popular items are often
placed in the middle of aisles, so we have to walk through the aisles to get what
C we want. Supermarkets also put expensive food at eye-level where they are easy
to reach. Cheaper items are placed on lower shelves, so we have to bend down
to get them. Cash registers are usually at the exit, so we have to walk through
the entire store before getting to the payment area. All of these strategies make
us see more food and spend more money.

Supermarkets use other techniques to control our shopping experience, too.
For example, they play music to affect how we shop. In a study of shopping
habits in a New York City supermarket, researchers found that slow music in a
D store makes us shop more slowly. In fact, when supermarkets play slow music
instead of fast music, shoppers spend about 38 percent more. Additionally, most
grocery stores don't have any clocks or windows. We can't look outside or see
what time it is while we shop. That way, we don't know how long we've been
shopping.

So what can you do to avoid buying more than you need? First, make a list
and don't buy anything that isn't on it. If you don't trust yourself to do this,
E bring only enough cash to buy what you need. Second, don't shop too often. Plan
several days of meals and shop for food only once or twice a week. Lastly, don't
shop when you're hungry. That's when everything in the store looks delicious!

Sometimes,
supermarkets
encourage shoppers
to buy food by giving
them samples to try.

UNDERSTANDING THE READING

A What is the main idea of the reading passage?

UNDERSTANDING
MAIN IDEAS

a. It has become more difficult for supermarkets to attract shoppers in recent years.

b. Supermarkets use certain methods to make shoppers spend more money.

c. There are some ways supermarket shoppers can avoid spending too much money.

B According to the reading, where are the following items usually placed? Note them on the diagram.

UNDERSTANDING DETAILS

> milk   fruit and vegetables   expensive cereal   cash registers   cheap cereal

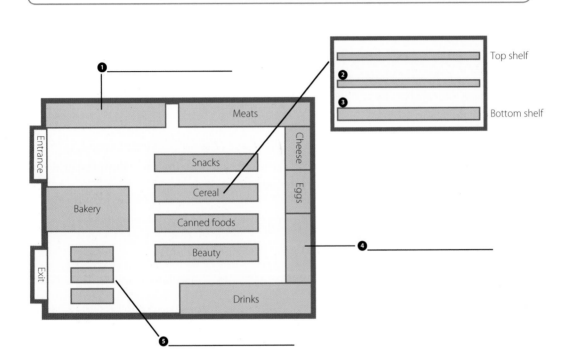

C Match the items in **B** to the reasons for where they are placed in a supermarket.

UNDERSTANDING PURPOSE

_____ 1. milk

_____ 2. cash registers

_____ 3. cheap cereal

_____ 4. expensive cereal

_____ 5. fruit and vegetables

a. to make the store front attractive

b. to make it easier to see and reach

c. to make it more difficult to reach

d. to make customers walk to the back of the store

e. to make customers walk through the entire store

> **CRITICAL THINKING**   As you read, try to **relate** the information to your own experience. Ask yourself: What information about the topic does the writer give? Does it match my own experience or situation?

D What's your local supermarket like? In what ways is it similar to or different from the one described? What do you think are the reasons for the differences? Discuss with a partner.

CRITICAL THINKING: RELATING IDEAS

DEVELOPING READING SKILLS

READING SKILL Identifying Supporting Ideas

Supporting ideas tell the reader more about the main idea of a paragraph. They can give specific examples of what the main idea means. They can also be reasons that explain the examples.

Read the following paragraph:

> From the moment we enter, a supermarket's floor plan controls the way we experience the store. There is usually only one way in and one way out, so we have to start and stop at particular places. Fruit and vegetables and the bakery are usually near the entrance. Fresh produce and the smell of bread baking can make a store seem fresh and attractive. This puts us in a good mood and makes us hungry, so we take our time and buy more food.

The blue sentence gives an example—**what** the design of supermarkets is usually like and **how** it controls the way people experience the store. The green sentences give reasons to support the example—**why** supermarkets are designed in that way.

IDENTIFYING SUPPORTING IDEAS **A** Read the topic sentence in the paragraph below. Underline the examples, and double underline the reasons that support the examples.

Supermarkets use various strategies to get customers to buy their products.

One way is placing products for children on lower shelves. This makes it easier

for children to see and then ask their parents to buy something. Another strategy

is giving out free food samples. Seeing, tasting, and smelling food can make people

feel hungry and want to buy it. Supermarkets also place candy and other cheap items

at the registers as customers might buy a snack while they wait in line.

CATEGORIZING **B** Is each sentence below a main idea or a supporting idea in the reading passage on pages 45–46? Write **M** for Main Idea or **S** for Supporting Idea.

1. The whole experience of shopping for food is planned and arranged for us. _____

2. Cheaper items are placed on lower shelves, so we have to bend down to get them. _____

3. Supermarkets use other techniques to control our shopping experience, too. _____

4. In fact, when supermarkets play slow music instead of fast music, shoppers spend about 38 percent more. _____

Video

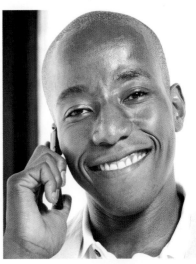

WHO DO YOU TRUST?

BEFORE VIEWING

A Look at the photos. Who do you think has the most persuasive face? Why? Discuss your ideas with a partner.   ANALYZING

B Read the information about Alex Todorov. Then check (✓) the sentences that Todorov is likely to agree with. Discuss your answers with a partner.   LEARNING ABOUT THE TOPIC

Psychology professor Alex Todorov studies how people make decisions. He's especially interested in how we evaluate people's personalities. He believes that people often make decisions about another person just by looking at their face. For example, we may decide whether or not the person is friendly, or whether we can trust them. Todorov's research also shows that people make these evaluations very quickly—in less than a second.

☐ 1. Our first impressions are usually influenced more by what people say than what they look like.

☐ 2. People usually decide within a short time if they will like someone.

☐ 3. When we see someone we don't know, we create an idea of them based on their appearance.

C The words in **bold** below are used in the video. Read the paragraph. Then match the correct form of each word or phrase to its definition.

One thing employers often want to know about a job seeker is if they are **competent** enough to do a good job. They also usually want to know if a person is **trustworthy**— whether or not you can depend on them. So how do they decide on the best person for the job? Experts say employers often make **judgments** just by looking at **candidates**. It's therefore important that job seekers present themselves well at the beginning of interviews, because people can form first impressions **in the blink of an eye**.

1. _____ (adj) honest; reliable

2. _____ (n) a decision

3. _____ (adv) very quickly

4. _____ (n) a person applying for a position

5. _____ (adj) having the necessary skills or qualities

WHILE VIEWING

A ▶ Watch the video. What does the experiment in the video show?

a. Most people are able to recognize smiles that aren't real.

b. Most people can guess the winner of an election by looking at their face.

c. Most people feel that what a politician does is more important than how they look.

B ▶ Watch the video again. Complete the sentences by circling the correct options.

1. According to Todorov, winning political candidates usually looked like they were _____.

   a. sociable and persuasive   b. skilled and honest

2. Todorov found that people seemed to trust people with faces that looked more _____.

   a. female   b. male

3. The experiment suggests that sometimes we may _____.

   a. make judgments based on feelings more than reason

   b. be able to tell whether someone is lying by looking at their face

AFTER VIEWING

A Did you choose the correct candidate each time? What helped you make your choices? Discuss with a partner.

B Work with a partner. Describe a time when your first impresssion of someone was inaccurate. What made you change your mind about them?

Reading 2

PREPARING TO READ

A Read the definitions of the words in blue. Then complete the sentences with the correct form of the words.

BUILDING VOCABULARY

> Something that is **natural** is not man-made.
>
> A **customer** is a person who buys something.
>
> If something is **probably** true, it is very likely to be true.
>
> When you **notice** something, you see or become aware of it.
>
> A person's **attitude** toward something is how they think and feel about it.
>
> A **message** is the main meaning of something that a person writes or says.
>
> If you can **influence** people, you can make them think a certain way.
>
> When there is a **limit** on something, there is a fixed level or amount allowed.

1. Successful businesses know how to attract _____.

2. Credit cards have a(n) _____ on the amount of money you can spend with them.

3. Positive online reviews can change people's _____ toward a certain product and _____ them to buy it.

4. A common _____ in advertisements is that a product is effective.

5. This product contains only _____ ingredients, so it's _____ good for your health.

6. Many shopping malls don't have windows, so people may not _____ how much time they spend in there.

B Discuss these questions with a partner.

USING VOCABULARY

1. Is there an interesting ad that you **noticed** recently? What was it?
2. What are some ways ads try to make people remember their **message**?

C Read the title and the first paragraph of the passage on pages 52–53. What do you think the passage is about? Then check your answer as you read.

PREDICTING

a. the importance of colors in product advertising
b. how advertising affects our shopping decisions
c. a comparison of various advertising strategies

THE POWER
OF PERSUASION

ADVERTISING STRATEGIES

- **Emotional Impact[3]:** Advertisers try to persuade us that their product will make us feel better, such as making us more attractive or loved.
- **Celebrity[4] Power:** Advertisers know that if we see a famous person using a product, we're more likely to buy it.
- **The Perfect Family:** Ads with happy families enjoying a product send a message: we can have the perfect family, too, if we buy the product.

CELEBRAT

A You're shopping, and you see two similar products. How do you decide which one to buy? You might think you make this decision by yourself—but this isn't always the case.

Don't believe it? Try this. What word is missing?

APPLE   TREE   GRASS   GR_____

B What was the first word you thought of? Did you think of "green"? That's **probably** because we **influenced** your answer. The words "tree" and "grass" made you think of the color green, right? The color of the words also influenced your decision. This is an example of priming.

C Psychologist Joshua Ackerman explains that priming is a way to "use cues[1] to influence your **attitudes** [and] responses, often without you even **noticing**." Priming speeds up our decision-making. That's why advertisers use it to persuade us to buy things.

INFLUENCING YOUR THINKING

D Use of color is one type of priming. Did you ever notice that a lot of signs and packaging use the color red? Studies show that red gives people warm and positive feelings. We feel good about products connected with the color red, so we want to buy them. Green, on the other hand, makes products seem **natural**. Food companies often use green packages to make their food seem healthy.

E Descriptions in ads and signs also influence buying decisions. For example, studies show that if an ad says there's a **limit** to the number of items you can buy, you'll want more of them. Why? According to psychologists, something becomes more attractive if it's rare.

F The sounds in ads also influence decision-making. For example, advertisers sometimes use rhymes[2] in their ads. In a study at the University of Texas, researchers showed people pairs of **messages** with the same meaning—one that rhymed and one that didn't. The study found that people are more likely to believe the rhyming message. Rhymes are also easier for people to remember, so when they go shopping, they're more likely to buy the product.

G Advertisers use a lot of techniques to persuade **customers** to buy their products. You might think you're in control when you shop, but maybe you're not. Priming strategies could be influencing your decisions.

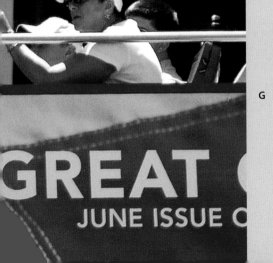

A bus passes by an ad for the movie *Shrek*.

---

[1]**cues:** signs or signals that tell you to do something
[3]**emotional impact:** If something has emotional impact, it affects the way you feel.

[2]**rhyme:** a set of words with similar sounds
[4]**celebrity:** a famous person

UNDERSTANDING THE READING

SUMMARIZING **A** Circle the correct words to complete the statement about priming.

Priming is a technique that [1] **advertisers / psychologists** use to persuade us to make [2] **careful / quick** buying decisions.

IDENTIFYING
MAIN IDEAS
B Read the sentences below. Check (✓) three that are main ideas of the passage.

☐ 1. People tend to buy more when they shop alone.

☐ 2. Priming is one way advertisers can influence people's decision-making.

☐ 3. Colors in ads can affect people's decisions to buy something.

☐ 4. Ads with photos are more likely to get people's attention.

☐ 5. The words and sounds that are used in ads can influence people's attitudes.

IDENTIFYING
SUPPORTING IDEAS
C Match the number of each main idea in exercise B to its supporting idea.

_____ a. People are more likely to buy something because of a rhyming ad.

_____ b. It makes people decide to buy something more quickly.

_____ c. Red and green often create good feelings in people.

UNDERSTANDING
DETAILS
D Match the priming strategies to their effects on customers.

Strategies: When ads …

_____ 1. use red

_____ 2. use green

_____ 3. limit the number we can buy

_____ 4. use rhymes

_____ 5. use celebrity power

Effects: We …

a. remember the product better

b. feel like we need to buy more

c. think a product is healthy

d. feel good about a product

e. think the product must be good because a famous person likes it

CRITICAL THINKING:
REFLECTING
E Look back at your answer to the question on page 51 about an interesting ad that you noticed (exercise B-1). What techniques did the ad use? Why did it influence you? Discuss with a partner.

Technique(s): _____

_____

Why it influenced you:

_____

_____

Writing

EXPLORING WRITTEN ENGLISH

A Read the information. Circle two words or phrases that show the order of ideas. Underline three words that introduce an additional piece of information.

NOTICING

According to Target Public Marketing—an American marketing company—successful ads have some common features:

- First of all, successful ads are unique and different from other ads of the same type.

- Good ads also get people's attention quickly.

- Another feature of effective ads is that they explain the benefits of a product clearly.

- Furthermore, the message in an ad needs to be simple and easy to remember.

- Finally, customers should have an easy way to buy the product, such as by clicking on the ad directly.

LANGUAGE FOR WRITING Connecting Ideas

As you learned in Unit 2, using words like *first* is one way to link ideas in a paragraph. The words and phrases below are used to connect ideas that don't need to go in any particular order.

> ***In addition / Furthermore / Also,*** *the use of celebrities in ads can make people buy products.*
> *Celebrities can **also** help reach a larger number of people.*
> ***Another*** *benefit of using a celebrity is that many people trust them.*

Note that we use commas after the adverbs that come at the beginning of a sentence.
Also can be placed before the main verb.
Another is an adjective and usually comes before a noun.

B Think of a product you use regularly and know well. Write three reasons why you like it.

Product: _____

Reasons:

1. _____

2. _____

3. _____

Now connect your reasons using suitable words or phrases from the Language for Writing box. Share your sentences with a partner.

_____

_____

_____

_____

_____

_____

_____

WRITING SKILL Writing Paragraphs and Topic Sentences

A topic sentence states the main idea of a paragraph. Topic sentences normally begin a paragraph, but they can also appear later. Example of a topic sentence:

Descriptions in ads and signs can influence buying decisions.

A paragraph is a group of sentences about one topic. All the sentences in a paragraph should relate to the topic or main idea of the paragraph. The sentences may give examples, facts, or reasons to help the reader clearly understand the main idea.

IDENTIFYING A
TOPIC SENTENCE

C Choose the most suitable topic sentence (a–c) for the paragraph below.

a. Supermarkets often arrange and organize their products in a specific way.

b. SuperFoods influences customers to spend more time in the store by having no windows or clocks.

c. SuperFoods is an example of a supermarket that uses strategies to make customers spend more money.

One technique the store uses is to put most of the basic food items, such as eggs and milk, at the back. Customers have to walk through the entire store to get to them. On the way, they may notice other products to buy. Another strategy SuperFoods uses is to put more expensive items on shelves at the customer's eye level. Less expensive brands are on the bottom shelves, so customers don't see them easily. This makes customers more likely to choose more expensive products. Finally, SuperFoods doesn't have any clocks or windows. It's hard for customers to know what time it is, so they tend to spend more time shopping in the store.

D Read the paragraph below and write a topic sentence for it.

WRITING A TOPIC
SENTENCE

_____

One way to buy less when you shop is to make a list of the things you need. If you plan carefully and only buy what's on the list, you'll spend less money. Another way to deal with supermarket strategies that make you buy more is to shop when you aren't hungry. Studies show that hungry shoppers buy more food than they need, so only go shopping after a meal. Shoppers can also save money by shopping for groceries online. If you shop at home, supermarket strategies, such as the layout of the store or free samples, won't influence your buying decisions.

E Read the topic sentence (in blue) in the paragraph below. Cross out two sentences that do not support the topic sentence.

IDENTIFYING
SUPPORTING IDEAS

Product packagers use color to influence people's buying decisions. (1) For example, packaging for children's cereals often use bright, primary colors such as red, blue, and yellow. (2) Studies show that children are more attracted to primary colors than lighter colors such as pink and white. (3) In addition, stores often put children's cereals on lower shelves so children will see them. (4) Another example is perfume packaging, where packagers often use colors such as gold or silver. (5) These colors make people think of expensive metals. (6) They also send the message that a product is valuable, so customers will feel good about paying a high price for it. (7) Perfume makers also put small bottles into large boxes so customers will think they are getting more of the product.

▼ **Perfume bottles are often designed to look valuable.**

WRITING TASK

GOAL You are going to write a paragraph on the following topic:
Choose a print ad and explain why it is effective. Give three reasons.

BRAINSTORMING **A** Find a print ad that you think is good. The ad should be selling a product or service. Then use the questions below to analyze it.

1. What does the ad say? What does it describe?
2. Are there any images in the ad?
3. How did the ad make you feel?
4. What other priming techniques does it use?

Now list reasons why the ad might influence people to pay for the product/service. Share your ideas with a partner.

_____

_____

_____

_____

PLANNING **B** Follow these steps to make notes for your paragraph. Don't worry about grammar or spelling. Don't write complete sentences.

Step 1 Look at your brainstorming ideas in exercise A. Choose the three best reasons for why the ad is effective.

Step 2 Order your reasons and note them in the outline as your supporting ideas.

Step 3 Write a topic sentence for your paragraph that tells the reader what you are going to discuss in the paragraph.

Step 4 Complete the outline with one detail to explain each supporting idea.

OUTLINE

Topic sentence: _____

Supporting Idea 1: _____

Detail: _____

Supporting Idea 2: _____

Detail: _____

Supporting Idea 3: _____

Detail: _____

FIRST DRAFT **C** Use the information in the outline to write a first draft of your paragraph.

REVISING PRACTICE

The drafts below are similar to the one you are going to write, but they are about an ad for a breakfast cereal.

What did the writer do in Draft 2 to improve the paragraph? Match the changes (a–d) to the highlighted parts.

a. added a detail for a supporting idea
b. improved the topic sentence
c. added a word or phrase to connect ideas
d. corrected a word or phrase that connects ideas

Draft 1

The ad for HyperHealth Cereal is very effective. First of all, the ad uses bright colors such as green, white, and blue. As a result, people interested in healthy eating are more likely to notice the product when they go to the supermarket. Then, the ad shows a group of happy people enjoying the cereal. This helps create positive feelings in customers about HyperHealth Cereal. There is an attractive couple featured in the ad. Advertisers know that customers are more likely to buy a product when the ad shows attractive people.

Draft 2

The ad for HyperHealth Cereal is very effective because it uses priming to influence customers to buy the product. First of all, the ad uses bright colors such as green, white, and blue. Studies show that people often think of "health" when they see these colors. As a result, people interested in healthy eating are more likely to notice the product when they go to the supermarket. The ad also shows a group of happy people enjoying the cereal. This helps create positive feelings in customers about HyperHealth Cereal. Finally, there is an attractive couple featured in the ad. Advertisers know that customers are more likely to buy a product when the ad shows attractive people.

☐

☐

☐

☐

D Now use the questions below to revise your paragraph.

REVISED DRAFT

☐ Did you write a topic sentence that describes the main idea of the paragraph?

☐ Do all of your sentences relate to the main idea?

☐ Did you use words and phrases that connect ideas?

☐ Did you include a detail for each supporting idea?

EDITING PRACTICE

Read the information below.

In sentences using connecting words and phrases, remember that:
- when *first, firstly,* or *first of all* come at the beginning of a sentence, they are followed by a comma.
- *also, another, furthermore,* and *in addition* introduce an idea that is not the first idea in a list or paragraph.
- *finally, furthermore,* and *in addition* come at the beginning of a sentence and are followed by a comma.
- a noun should come after *another* or *an additional*; e.g., *Another reason is … / An additional problem is … .*
- *finally* and *lastly* introduce the last idea.

Correct one mistake with connecting words and phrases in each of the sentences (1–4).

1. Ads use firstly emotional impact to make us believe that their product will affect our lives in a good way.

2. One technique is to place items in certain positions on the shelves. An additional is to use colors to affect the way we feel about a product.

3. Some ads use celebrities, furthermore.

4. Finally ads should have clear messages that are easy to understand.

FINAL DRAFT **E** Follow these steps to write a final draft.

1. Check your revised draft for mistakes with words and phrases that connect ideas.

2. Now use the checklist on page 218 to write a final draft. Make any other necessary changes.

UNIT REVIEW
Answer the following questions.

1. What is one way advertisers persuade customers to buy their product?

_____

_____

_____

2. What does a topic sentence do in a paragraph?

_____

_____

_____

3. Do you remember the meanings of these words? Check (✓) the ones you know. Look back at the unit and review the ones you don't know.

Reading 1:
☐ attractive ☐ avoid ☐ cash
☐ control ☐ instead of ☐ percent **AWL**
☐ product ☐ store ☐ strategy **AWL**
☐ trust

Reading 2:
☐ attitude **AWL** ☐ customer ☐ influence
☐ limit ☐ message ☐ natural
☐ notice ☐ probably

GREEN LIVING 4

A family surrounded by the trash they produced in a week

THINK AND DISCUSS

1 Why do you think the photographer took the image above?

2 What do people usually do with trash in your community?

DEALING WITH TRASH

Adventurer Alison Teal travels the world making films about environmental issues. Once, she went to Thilafushi, or "Trash Island," in the

What do you do with your trash? Instead of throwing it away, some people do something different with their garbage.

1. _____: Collecting trash helped 14-year-old Willow Tufano buy a house. Willow **collected** things on her sidewalk that people didn't want anymore, such as furniture and electronics. She then sold the items on the Internet. With the money she earned, she and her mother bought an inexpensive house in Port Charlotte, Florida.

2. _____: Instead of burying trash in a landfill,[1] Sweden burns it to produce energy for homes and businesses. In fact, Sweden is so good at using trash that it doesn't have enough now—so it imports[2] trash from other countries.

3. _____: In 2012, blogger Lauren Singer decided to live a zero-waste lifestyle by **recycling** and composting[3] all her trash. In three years of living a zero-waste lifestyle, she was able to fit all her non-recyclable trash in a small glass container.

[1]**landfill:** a place where garbage is buried under the ground
[2]**import:** to bring products from one country into another country
[3]**composting:** using garbage, such as food waste, to grow plants

Lauren Singer could fit three years of trash in a small jar.

Reading 1

PREPARING TO READ

BUILDING
VOCABULARY

A The words and phrases in blue below are used in the reading passage on pages 65–66. Read the paragraphs. Then match the correct form of each word or phrase to its definition.

Trash on land and in the sea can **cause** serious problems for both humans and animals. Plastic garbage, for example, can **float** in the ocean for years and **kill** birds and fish when they eat it by mistake. Although one way of handling the problem is to **clean up** the ocean and landfills, a more effective **solution** is to reduce the amount we produce.

Many cities have programs to make people **aware** of the problem. For example, San Francisco has a zero-waste program. Signs throughout the city show which types of materials are suitable for recycling. The SF Environment website **reports** that if people recycle correctly, the city can reduce landfill waste by 90 percent.

1. _____ (v) to make happen

2. _____ (adj) knowing about something

3. _____ (v) to end someone's or something's life

4. _____ (n) an answer to a problem

5. _____ (v) to write or speak formally about something

6. _____ (v) to move in the air or on top of a liquid, such as water

7. _____ (v) to remove dirty or unwanted things completely

USING
VOCABULARY

B Discuss these questions with a partner.

1. Does garbage **cause** any problems in your community?

2. Have you ever helped out in **cleaning up** your school or community?

BRAINSTORMING

C What kinds of everyday items are made of plastic? Share your ideas with a partner.

_____

_____

PREDICTING

D Read the title of the passage and the first paragraph on page 65. What do you think is in the island? How did it get to the middle of the ocean? Discuss with a partner. Then check your ideas as you read the passage.

Pieces of plastic trash collected from the Great Pacific Garbage Patch

GARBAGE ISLAND

🎧 7

A   You can't see it from the air. It's almost impossible to see from a ship. But somewhere in the North Pacific is a giant island of garbage, **floating** just below the ocean's surface.

HOW DID IT GET THERE?

B   The garbage island is not really an island. It's a collection of millions of pieces of plastic and other objects that people have **thrown away**, such as shopping bags and water bottles. Pacific Ocean currents bring the objects together and **cause** them to spin around in a giant circle. The spinning movement stops the garbage from escaping. New objects enter the spinning water, and the island grows larger.

C   No one really knows how big the island is. Some scientists say it is about 270,000 square miles (700,000 square kilometers). Some studies **report** that it may be up to 20 times larger—twice the size of the continental United States.

WHAT PROBLEMS DOES IT CAUSE?

D   The larger pieces of garbage in the island are a problem for wildlife. For example, sea turtles often think plastic bags are jellyfish—their favorite food. They eat the plastic and die. Seabirds looking for food in the ocean may also die from eating plastic objects floating on the water.

E   In addition, tiny pieces of plastic near the ocean surface block sunlight from reaching deeper water. The lack of sunlight kills very small sea organisms[1] called plankton. As a result, there is less food for larger fish, such as tuna.

WHAT CAN WE DO?

F   Cleaning up a giant island of plastic garbage isn't easy, but there may be some solutions. One method is to use technology to collect the trash and recycle it. Environmental engineer Cesar Harada is building a type of robot boat that gathers up trash. Harada hopes this robot technology will help reduce garbage in the Pacific.

G   New approaches to recycling can also help make more people aware of the problem. For example, singer and songwriter Pharrell Williams works with a company that recycles plastic garbage to make denim[2] for blue jeans. In this way, he combines his interest in fashion with his concern for the environment. If many people make small changes, it can have a big impact. As Williams says, "The ocean is just one part of the Earth … but the world is made up of 75 to 80 percent water. It's a huge place to start."

[1] **organisms:** living things
[2] **denim:** a strong fabric made of cotton, usually used in jeans

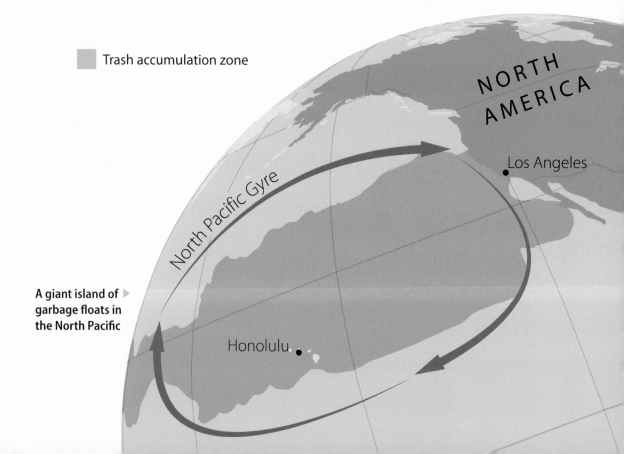

Trash accumulation zone

North Pacific Gyre

NORTH AMERICA

Los Angeles

Honolulu

A giant island of ▶ garbage floats in the North Pacific

UNDERSTANDING THE READING

A What is the main idea of the passage?

    a. Scientists are planning a huge project to clean up garbage in the Pacific Ocean.

    b. A garbage island in the Pacific Ocean is causing environmental problems, and some people are helping to reduce it.

    c. There is an island of garbage in the Pacific Ocean, and nobody knows where it came from.

B Circle the correct words to complete the summary.

There is an island in the Pacific that is made up of different kinds of trash. Most of the garbage patch is actually tiny pieces of [1] **plastic / food**. The objects in the island are always moving [2] **in a circle / toward land**. The movement of water [3] **attracts new objects / pushes objects away**, so the island is always getting [4] **smaller / bigger**. Experts aren't sure how large the island is, but some think that it could be [5] **double / three times** the size of the United States.

C Complete the diagram about the problems with trash in the ocean.

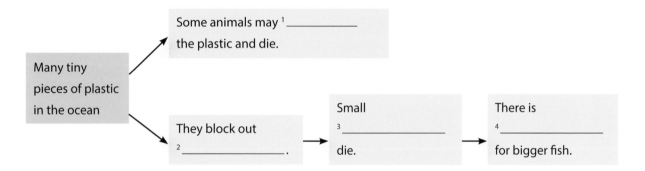

Some animals may [1] _____ the plastic and die.

Many tiny pieces of plastic in the ocean

They block out [2] _____.

Small [3] _____ die.

There is [4] _____ for bigger fish.

> **CRITICAL THINKING**   When you describe **problems and solutions**, it is common to present the problem first and then possible solutions. As you read, ask yourself: What evidence does the writer give to explain the problem? Do the solutions clearly match the problem?

D Complete the possible solutions to ocean trash mentioned in the passage. Then discuss with a partner: What other things could people do to help reduce the problem?

Cesar Harada: cleaning up ocean trash using a(n) _____

Pharrell Williams: _____ plastic trash into clothes and making people _____ of the problem

DEVELOPING READING SKILLS

READING SKILL Scanning for Details

Scanning helps you find important details quickly. When you scan, you move your eyes quickly over the reading and look for specific things. For example, you can scan for **numbers** to find times, dates, and distances. You can look for **capitalized words** to find names of people and places. You can also identify **nouns** and **verbs** that appear several times because they are likely to be important.

IDENTIFYING **A** Read the questions below. What kind of information do you need to scan for in each case? Use the words from the box. Some words can be used more than once.

> year   name   place   number

1. Who discovered the garbage island? _____

2. When did he discover the island? _____

3. Where was he sailing to when he found it? _____

4. When did he use drones to do research on the island? _____

5. How long in meters were some of the plastic islands? _____

SCANNING FOR DETAILS **B** Scan the following paragraph and find answers to the questions above.

A racing-boat captain named Charles Moore first discovered the garbage island in 1997. He was sailing from Hawaii to California after competing in a boat race. As Moore crossed the North Pacific, he noticed many pieces of plastic around his boat. As an oceanographer, Moore decided to study the island. In 1999, he found that there was six times more plastic in the area than plankton. In 2014, he used drones to help measure the amount of trash in the island. He and his team also discovered there was 100 times more garbage in the island than previously recorded. They also found some more permanent plastic islands that were more than 15 meters long.

1. _____   2. _____   3. _____

4. _____   5. _____

Captain Charles Moore ▶
showing plastic waste
collected from the
garbage island

Video

TRASH PEOPLE

▲ Trash People in
Zermatt, Switzerland

BEFORE VIEWING

A Look at the photo and the caption. What are the "Trash People"? Why do you think they were created? Discuss with a partner.

PREDICTING

B Read the information about trash around the world. Answer the questions below. Then share your ideas with a partner.

LEARNING ABOUT
THE TOPIC

Globally, we produce over 1.3 billion tons of trash a year—the weight of about 3,500 Empire State Buildings. Of this amount, only about 1 percent is recycled. Most of the world's trash comes from cities, so managing the problem is likely to be more difficult as more people move to cities. According to a World Bank report, the number of people living in cities in 2025 will be the same as the total world population in 2000.

1. Roughly how many tons of trash are produced each year?

   _____

2. Why do you think so little trash is recycled?

   _____

3. In your view, why are growing cities a problem?

   _____

C The words in **bold** below are used in the video. Read the paragraph. Then match the correct form of the words to their definitions.

After we throw our trash away, **garbage collectors** transport it in large trucks. Each truck then goes to a garbage processing center where some of the trash is recycled and the rest goes to a landfill. An artist named HA Schult works to **transform** landfill trash into **sculptures**. He **sets up** his art in cities all over the world.

1. _____ (n) a solid piece of art

2. _____ (v) to change one thing to another thing

3. _____ (n) a person who takes trash from people's homes

4. _____ (v) to put things in position

WHILE VIEWING

A ▶ Watch the video. Circle the correct answers.

1. The main aim of HA Schult's project is to show people that _____.

   a. garbage is a big problem   b. you can turn anything into art

2. Schult thinks that problems with trash are _____.

   a. the same in every country   b. worse in poor countries

B ▶ Watch the video again. According to the video, which countries have Schult's sculptures been to?

a. Egypt

b. China

c. Russia

d. the United States

e. South Africa

f. Switzerland

g. Germany

h. France

AFTER VIEWING

A Complete the chart. Check (✓) the people who match the descriptions.

	Cesar Harada	Pharrell Williams	HA Schult
1. deals with ocean trash			
2. turns garbage into art			
3. uses robot technology to reduce the problem of trash			
4. turns trash into something you can use every day			

B Work with a partner. If Schult's sculptures were going to be on display in your city, where would be the best place to put them? Why?

I think it would be best to put them _____ because

_____

Reading 2

PREPARING TO READ

A The words and phrases in **blue** below are used in the reading passage on pages 72–73. Complete each sentence with the correct form of the word or phrase.

BUILDING VOCABULARY

> A **painting** is a colored drawing.
>
> An **image** is a picture.
>
> When you **deal with** something, you do something about it.
>
> When you **create** something, you make it.
>
> **Material** is something you use to make things.
>
> If you **receive** something, you get it from someone.
>
> If you feel **proud**, you feel pleased about something you did.
>
> An **organization** is an official group of people, such as a company.

1. *Mona Lisa* is perhaps Leonardo Da Vinci's most famous _____.

2. A(n) _____ called The Ocean Cleanup is working to remove plastic from the oceans' garbage patches.

3. Countries must work together to _____ environmental problems such as pollution in the ocean.

4. HA Schult uses many types of _____—such as paper, glass, plastic, and metal—to _____ his sculptures.

5. Social media sites such as Instagram and Flickr allow people to upload and share _____.

6. When people help clean up garbage from parks and beaches, they can feel _____ of the work they are doing.

7. Artist Roy Lichtenstein _____ many awards for his works of art.

B Discuss these questions with a partner.

USING VOCABULARY

1. What environmental **organizations** do you know?

2. What kinds of issues do they **deal with**?

C Read the first paragraph of the passage on page 72. What kind of art do you think Vik Muniz makes? Discuss with a partner. Then check your ideas as you read the passage.

PREDICTING

THE ART OF RECYCLING

A Brazilian artist Vik Muniz uses everyday objects in unusual ways. Through his art, Muniz makes people think differently about their everyday lives—even their own garbage.

B In 2007, Muniz worked on a two-year project at one of the world's largest landfills. Until its closure in 2012, Jardim Gramacho **received** about 70 percent of the garbage from Rio de Janeiro. About 3,000 garbage pickers, known as *catadores*, worked there. Their job was to hunt through the garbage for recyclable cans, bottles, and other materials. They then made money by selling the objects to recycling companies.

C The catadores' work was dirty and dangerous, and most of them only received between $20 and $25 a day. Despite the hard conditions, many catadores were **proud** of their work. Valter Dos Santos, a worker at Jardim Gramacho for more than 25 years, told Muniz: "I am proud to be a picker. I try to explain to people [that recycling prevents] great harm to nature and the environment. People sometimes say, 'But one single [soda] can?' One single can is of great importance! [T]hat single can will make the difference."

D Muniz became friends with Dos Santos and other catadores. They allowed him to take their photographs at the landfill, where they posed[1] for artistic portraits. For example, Muniz photographed a landfill worker in the style of a famous French **painting**, *The Death of Marat*. The workers then helped Muniz **create** huge **images** of these photos on the floor of his studio. They used **material** from the landfill to add color and depth to the images.

E Why create such huge images using garbage? Muniz says he wanted to "change the lives of people with the same materials they **deal with** every day." A photograph of his recreation of the French painting sold for £28,000 ($50,000) at a London art auction. Muniz gave the money to the catadores workers' **organization**.

F In 2010, British-Brazilian director Lucy Walker created a movie about Muniz's project called *Waste Land*. The film received many awards and helped make people aware of the garbage collectors' lives. The catadores also began to see themselves differently. "Sometimes we see ourselves as so small," says Irma, a cook at Gramacho, "but people out there see us as so big, so beautiful."

---

[1] **pose:** to get your body into a certain position for a photo, painting, etc.

Workers at Jardim Gramacho picked waste to earn money for their families.

UNDERSTANDING THE READING

UNDERSTANDING
PURPOSE

A Match each paragraph from the reading passage to its purpose.

_____ 1. Paragraph B   a. to describe the impact of Muniz's project

_____ 2. Paragraph C   b. to describe how Muniz carried out his project

_____ 3. Paragraph D   c. to give information about the catadores' jobs

_____ 4. Paragraph E   d. to show how catadores feel about their work

_____ 5. Paragraph F   e. to explain why Muniz did his project

SCANNING FOR
DETAILS

B Scan the passage and write a short answer to each question.

1. What was Jardim Gramacho?	
2. Where was it?	
3. How many people worked there?	
4. What did these people do?	
5. How much did they earn?	

SEQUENCING

C Put the events describing Muniz's project in the order they happened (1–6).

_____ a. Muniz became close to a few catadores.

_____ b. Muniz took a photo of the recreated artwork in his studio.

_____ c. Muniz sold the photograph at an auction.

_____ d. The catadores worked with Muniz to create a large image using trash items.

_____ e. Muniz gave the money to the catadores' work organization.

_____ f. Muniz took a picture of a catador lying in the same position as a person in a French painting.

CRITICAL THINKING:
INFERRING MEANING

D Read the quote from Valter Dos Santos. What do you think he means? Discuss your ideas with a partner.

"One single can is of great importance! [T]hat single can will make the difference."

a. Many small actions, when you add them all up, can have a big effect.

b. Selling one can to a recycling company can help a catador earn money.

c. There are certain materials in the garbage pile that are worth a lot more money than others.

Writing

EXPLORING WRITTEN ENGLISH

A Circle the correct word to complete each sentence.

NOTICING

1. The larger pieces of garbage in the island are a **problem** / **solution** for wildlife.
2. A giant island of plastic garbage is a **problem** / **solution**, but there may be a **problem** / **solution**.
3. Trash on land and in the sea can cause serious **problems** / **solutions** such as water pollution.
4. One **problem** / **solution** is to clean up the ocean and landfills.
5. Another **problem** / **solution** is to reduce the amount of garbage we produce.

LANGUAGE FOR WRITING Stating Problems and Proposing Solutions

You can use certain words and phrases to introduce problems and propose solutions.

In a problem/solution paragraph, it is more common to introduce the problem first:

X is a problem, but there may be some solutions.
X can cause problems for Y, but there are some possible solutions.
There is/are [description of problem], but we may be able to solve this problem.

You can then propose solutions in the rest of the paragraph. It is common to use an infinitive phrase after these expressions:

One solution/idea/answer is ... (e.g., to bring your own bag)
Another solution/idea/answer is ... (e.g., to buy only what you need)

Use a base verb after *can*:

In addition, we can tell others about the problem.

B Complete the sentences with suitable phrases from the box above.

Today, electronic waste (e-waste) is one of the most common types of trash. It includes things like cell phones, televisions, and computers. E-waste is especially a problem in Asia. Between 2010 and 2015, the amount of e-waste produced in the region increased by more than 60 percent. The growing amount of e-waste can cause [1]_____ the environment, but there may be some solutions. [2]_____ to create a system for recycling e-waste, since burning or burying e-waste is harmful to the environment. [3]_____ to reuse old electronic devices by sending them to developing countries.

C Think about a problem in your school or neighborhood as well as two possible solutions. Make notes in the box provided. Then write sentences about your ideas using the phrases in the Language for Writing box.

Example:

Problem: not enough streetlights near home

Solution: speak to council, talk to neighbors

Problems in My School / Neighborhood	Possible Solutions

_____

_____

_____

_____

_____

_____

_____

WRITING SKILL Using Supporting Sentences

As you saw in Unit 3, paragraphs usually have one main idea. The main idea is expressed in a topic sentence. The rest of the sentences in the paragraph support and help explain the main idea.

There are two types of supporting sentences:

Supporting ideas expand on the main idea. They can be in different forms, such as reasons, examples, or steps in a process.

Supporting details expand on supporting ideas. Like supporting ideas, they can be in different forms such as facts, examples, or explanations.

Supporting sentences must relate to the topic sentence. You can link supporting sentences with the connecting words and phrases you studied in Units 2 and 3.

D Underline the three supporting ideas (solutions) in this paragraph.

IDENTIFYING SUPPORTING IDEAS

My city faces air pollution and traffic jams because of the high number of cars on the road, but there may be some ways to improve the situation. One approach is to encourage people to take public transportation. We can have more buses and trains, or create more bicycle lanes. Another way is to increase the cost of driving. For example, we can make parking more expensive or make people pay to drive into the city center. In addition, we can make residents aware of the importance of caring about the environment. For instance, we can have "car-free" days where people travel by other forms of transportation.

E Check (✓) three supporting ideas for the topic sentence below.

IDENTIFYING SUPPORTING IDEAS

Topic sentence: People in my city don't recycle very much, but there are a few ways we could get more people involved in recycling.

☐ 1. Some people use trash to create artworks.

☐ 2. Schools can teach students how to separate their trash for recycling.

☐ 3. San Francisco has a very successful recycling program.

☐ 4. We can have more recycling bins to make it convenient for people.

☐ 5. The city can give people rewards for recycling their trash.

F Now write a detail for each supporting idea in exercise E. Then share your sentences with a partner.

WRITING SUPPORTING DETAILS

1. _____

_____

2. _____

_____

3. _____

_____

WRITING TASK

GOAL You are going to write a paragraph on the following topic:

Choose an environmental issue and propose how people can help improve the situation.

A Work with a partner. Brainstorm two environmental problems in your community or in the world. Then think of as many solutions as possible for each one. Write your ideas in the chart.

Problems	Possible Solutions

B Follow these steps to make notes for your paragraph. Don't worry about grammar or spelling. Don't write complete sentences.

Step 1 Choose the problem from exercise A with the best solutions.

Step 2 Write a topic sentence for your paragraph that states the problem.

Step 3 Choose the three best solutions and note them as your supporting ideas in the outline.

Step 4 For each solution, list at least one detail (e.g., example, fact, explanation).

OUTLINE

Topic sentence: _____

_____

Supporting idea 1: _____

_____

Detail: _____

Supporting idea 2: _____

_____

Detail: _____

Supporting idea 3: _____

_____

Detail: _____

C Use the information in your outline to write a first draft of your paragraph.

REVISING PRACTICE

The drafts below are similar to the one you are going to write, but they are on a different topic:

Plastic causes problems for the environment. What can we do to improve this situation?

What did the writer do in Draft 2 to improve the paragraph? Match the changes (a–d) to the highlighted parts.

a. deleted an idea that is not needed

b. improved a supporting idea

c. added a detail to a supporting idea

d. introduced a problem/solution in a clearer way

Draft 1

Plastic garbage is a problem for the environment, but there are some possible solutions. Discourage people from buying drinks in plastic bottles. Instead, they can buy reusable bottles made of glass or metal. This is a good way to save money. Another solution is to get people to bring their own shopping bags to stores. In addition, don't store food in plastic wrap. They can keep leftovers in reusable glass containers instead.

Draft 2

Plastic garbage is a problem for the environment, but there are some possible solutions. One solution is to discourage people from buying drinks in plastic bottles. Instead, they can buy reusable bottles made of glass or metal. Another solution is to get people to bring their own shopping bags to stores. That way they won't use the stores' plastic bags. In addition, people should stop using plastic wrap to store their food. They can keep leftovers in reusable glass containers instead.

☐
☐
☐
☐

D Now use the questions below to revise your paragraph.   REVISED DRAFT

☐ Did you include a topic sentence?

☐ Did you include three supporting ideas?

☐ Did you introduce the problem and solutions clearly?

☐ Do all your sentences relate to the main idea?

☐ Did you include at least one detail to explain each supporting idea?

EDITING PRACTICE

Read the information below.

In sentences that introduce problems and propose solutions, remember to:
- use a comma before *but* in a sentence that introduces a problem.
- use an infinitive phrase after *One/Another solution is*.
- use the base form of a verb after *can* when introducing a solution.

Correct one mistake with expressions for introducing problems and proposing solutions in each of the sentences (1–8).

1. Air pollution is a problem but there are some possible solutions.

2. One solution is reduce the number of cars on the roads.

3. Another solution is to talking to factory owners.

4. Also, we can using public transportation instead of driving.

5. My town has a problem with trash on the streets but there are some ways to improve the situation.

6. One idea is have more trash cans.

7. Another solution is to telling people about the problem.

8. In addition, we can tries to recycle more.

FINAL DRAFT   **E**   Follow these steps to write a final draft.

1. Check your revised draft for mistakes with expressions for introducing problems and proposing solutions.

2. Now use the checklist on page 218 to write a final draft. Make any other necessary changes.

UNIT REVIEW

Answer the following questions.

1. Which idea in this unit do you think is the most effective way of reducing trash?

_____

_____

_____

2. What do you do when you scan a reading passage?

_____

_____

_____

3. Do you remember the meanings of these words? Check (✔) the ones you know. Look back at the unit and review the ones you don't know.

Reading 1:

☐ aware [AWL]   ☐ cause   ☐ clean up

☐ collect   ☐ float   ☐ kill

☐ recycle   ☐ report   ☐ solution

☐ throw away

Reading 2:

☐ create [AWL]   ☐ deal with   ☐ image [AWL]

☐ material   ☐ organization   ☐ painting

☐ proud   ☐ receive

FOOD JOURNEYS 5

**Freshly picked hyacinth beans,
West Bengal, India**

THINK AND DISCUSS

1 What do you see in the photo? Do people eat this kind of food in your country?
2 Skim through the unit. What types of food do you see?

A Read the information on these pages and answer the questions.

1. What do the photos show? Have you tried any food from these places?
2. Think about De Los Santos's questions for the photographers. Describe a picture that you might take to show these things.

B Match the words in blue words to their definitions.

_____ (adj) usual or common; something you expect

_____ (v) to use or experience with others

_____ (n) the ideas or behavior of a people or society

THE WORLD ON A PLATE

Food photographer Penny De Los Santos believes that photos can tell powerful stories. So she gave photographers an assignment: Take a picture that shows the role of food in your culture.

De Los Santos told the photographers to think about the answers to these questions: What's a typical food scene in your world? What do your friends and family do when they eat together? How do they share meals?

De Los Santos received thousand of photos from photographers all over the world. She evaluated each one based on its color, lighting, composition (form), and story. Here are some of her favorites.

On a cold morning in Harbin, China, a woman prepares fresh steamed mantou (a bread-like bun).

A villager carries a tray of fruits and nuts during a festival in Iran.

Ingredients for brinjal curry, India

A family in Cambodia enjoys fresh pineapples.

Reading 1

PREPARING TO READ

A The words in **blue** below are used in the reading passage on pages 85–86. Read the paragraph. Then match the correct form of each word to its definition.

Many **types** of edible plants—plants you can eat—grow in Mediterranean countries such as Italy and Greece. Sometimes these plants—herbs, vegetables, and fruits—grow near people's homes. People often **pick** them, take them home, and use them right away. This way, they are still very **fresh**. One fruit in particular, the olive, grows well in the Mediterranean climate, so people use a lot of olive oil there. The oil has a good **taste**, so people often pour it right on their food. They also use it to **prepare** food. For example, if you visit a Mediterranean home, someone might **offer** you **fried** fish cooked in olive oil and a salad of fresh vegetables mixed with the oil.

1. _____ (v) to make something, such as food

2. _____ (n) a kind or a category

3. _____ (adj) cooked in fat, such as butter or oil

4. _____ (adj) recently made or produced; not old

5. _____ (v) to give something to someone

6. _____ (v) to take or remove something by breaking it off

7. _____ (n) flavor, e.g., fruity, sweet

B Discuss these questions with a partner.

1. What **types** of edible plants grow where you live?

2. Do you eat a lot of **fried** food? Why or why not?

3. What kinds of food do you **offer** people when they come to your home?

C What are some typical dishes in your country or culture? Make a list and share your ideas with a partner.

1. _____   2. _____   3. _____

4. _____   5. _____   6. _____

D The reading on pages 85–86 is about a trip that photographer Matthieu Paley made. Look at the photos and read the captions. Then discuss with a partner: What place is the passage mainly about? What kind of food do people eat there?

I think it's mainly about …

People probably eat … there.

A family in Crete gathers for lunch. The Mediterranean diet is one of the oldest diets still popular today.

A GLOBAL FOOD JOURNEY

🎧 9

A   In 2014, French photographer Matthieu Paley set out to explore the world of food. His travels took him through jungles, over mountains, and beneath the sea. He went on the journey to explore how our environment affects the food we eat—and how our diet[1] shapes our **culture**. Paley **shared** his experiences in a visual food diary, called *We Are What We Eat*.

During his journey, Paley visited six countries around the world to experience their food and culture.

B   Paley saw how food plays an important role in people's lives all over the world. In Greenland, he went seal hunting with the Inuit to catch food for dinner. He gathered honey from trees with the Hazda people of Tanzania. And in Malaysian Borneo, he went diving to catch sea urchins[2] and octopuses.

C   In Crete—the largest island in Greece—Paley enjoyed a **typical** Mediterranean family meal. On the following page is an excerpt from his diary.

[1] **diet:** the food that we often eat
[2] **sea urchin:** a small sea animal with a round shell and sharp spikes

APRIL 2014

D
I am at the Moschonas' home for their Saturday family gathering. Everyone was working in the fields this afternoon, and there is a pile of **fresh** wild herbs on the table. The family welcomes me, and the conversation is loud and lively. I feel right at home.

E
"Now, we make kalitsounia!" says Stella. These are small **fried** pies filled with wild herbs called horta. In Crete, April has been a time to **pick** horta for thousands of years. Stella **prepares** dough[3] on the table. She cuts it into small squares and wraps the herbs. Then she fries the little pies in olive oil.

F
Someone takes a large bucket of snails from the freezer. The Moschonas eat snails all year round. They are probably the oldest food eaten by humans. Snails may also be the easiest to catch, because you just go for a walk, turn over some rocks, and there they are.

[3]**dough**: a mixture of flour and water, often used for baking

G
"And they are full of Omega 3,[4] no fat on that meat either!" Stella says. She'll prepare the snails with a thick sauce. She **offers** me a kalitsounia, hot out of the pan.

H
"Tell me about the horta," I ask. "What did you pick today?"

I
Leaning over the table, Stella says with a smile, "Oh, there are over 20 **types** of herbs out there, if you know where to find them. And I know them all by name!"

J
My plate is filled with snails. On the table, there are also beans, small fried fish, and another vegetable. It looks like tiny asparagus, and has a bitter **taste**. Manolis sits next to me. He points at the dish. "This one is medicament. Medicine!" He says, "Eat a ton of it!" I try it. "We call these avronies … only in this season," he says. "You are a lucky man!"

[4]**Omega 3**: a type of fatty acid that is good for health

A typical Cretan meal of snails, sardines, and fava beans

UNDERSTANDING THE READING

A Complete the summary of the main ideas of the passage.

SUMMARIZING

a. a diary   b. a typical Mediterranean meal   c. pictures

d. the food people eat   e. the world   f. to Crete

In 2014, Matthieu Paley went on a trip around [1]_____. He wanted to learn about the connection between [2]_____ and where they live. Paley took [3]_____ and kept [4]_____ to record his experiences. In one entry, he described his visit [5]_____, where he had [6]_____.

B What does the writer express in the following paragraphs? Circle the best choice.

UNDERSTANDING MAIN IDEAS

1. Paragraph D   why he traveled to Crete / how he felt at the dinner

2. Paragraph E   how Stella prepares kalitsounia / what kalitsounia tastes like

3. Paragraph F   a food with a long history / a dish with a strange taste

4. Paragraph J   Paley's meal at the Moschonas' / Paley's next food journey

C Match the types of food (1–5) with the descriptions. One type of food is extra.

UNDERSTANDING DETAILS

_____ 1. kalitsounias   a. vegetables that look like small asparagus

_____ 2. horta   b. wild greens that people pick in April

_____ 3. snails   c. probably one of the oldest food people eat

_____ 4. fried fish   d. small pies filled with edible plants

_____ 5. avronies

> **CRITICAL THINKING**   **Justifying** means explaining the reasons for your opinion or preference. For example, when you evaluate something, think about why and how you made your decision.

D Look at the foods from Matthieu Paley's diary. How much would you like to try each one? Give each a number (1–3) and write a reason.

CRITICAL THINKING: JUSTIFYING YOUR OPINION

1 = I don't want to try it.   ⟶   3 = I really want to try it.

kalitsounia   1   2   3   _____

snails   1   2   3   _____

avronies   1   2   3   _____

Cretan kalitsounia

DEVELOPING READING SKILLS

READING SKILL Recognizing Pronoun References

Pronouns usually refer to nouns that appear earlier in a text. The pronoun may refer to a noun earlier in the same sentence or in a previous sentence.

A subject pronoun usually refers to a subject mentioned earlier.

Matthieu Paley set out on a food journey in 2014, and he visited six countries.
　　　subject　　　　　　　　　　　　　　　　　　　subject pronoun

Similarly, an object pronoun usually refers to an object mentioned earlier:

Someone took a bucket of snails from the freezer and put it on the table.
　　　　　　　　object　　　　　　　　　　　　　　object pronoun

Note: Pronouns always match the nouns they refer to in number and in gender.

ANALYZING **A** Underline the subject and object pronouns in the following paragraph. Then draw an arrow to the noun that each pronoun refers to.

Food tourists travel just to explore food in different countries. When food tourists take a tour, they choose a place that has the type of food they want to explore. For example, food tourists might go to China and take cooking classes. Food experts might take the travelers to markets and help them buy fresh ingredients. In Mediterranean countries such as Spain and Italy, travelers can have farmhouse vacations. They stay on farms and learn about the local diet. They also help farmers pick fruit and vegetables and learn how to prepare them using local recipes.

IDENTIFYING PRONOUN REFERENCE **B** The sentences below are from the passage on page 86. Write the word(s) that each underlined pronoun refers to.

1. Paragraph **E**: Stella prepares dough on the table. <u>She</u> cuts <u>it</u> into small squares and wraps the herbs.

   She = _____　　　　　　　it = _____

2. Paragraph **F**: Snails may also be the easiest to catch, because you just go for a walk, turn over some rocks, and there <u>they</u> are.

   they = _____

3. Paragraph **I**: Leaning over the table, Stella says with a smile, "Oh, there are over 20 types of herbs out there, if you know where to find <u>them</u>. And I know <u>them</u> all by name!"

   them = _____　　　　　　them = _____

4. Paragraph **J**: On the table, there are also beans, small fried fish, and another vegetable. <u>It</u> looks like tiny asparagus, and has a bitter taste.

   It = _____

Video

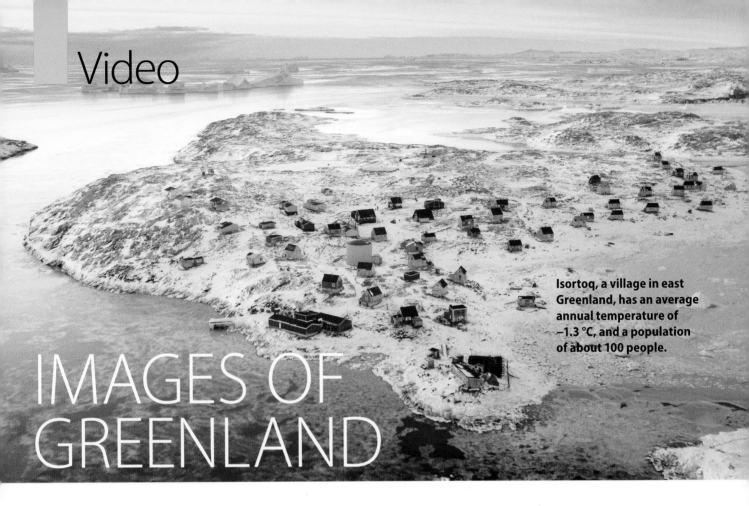

IMAGES OF GREENLAND

Isortoq, a village in east Greenland, has an average annual temperature of −1.3 °C, and a population of about 100 people.

BEFORE VIEWING

A Look at the photo caption and the title of the video. What do you think is a typical diet for someone living in this place? Discuss your ideas with a partner.

PREDICTING

B Read the information about Greenland and the Inuit culture. Then answer the questions.

LEARNING ABOUT THE TOPIC

The Inuit live in the Arctic regions of Greenland, Canada, and Alaska in the United States. Traditionally, they eat mostly meat because it is impossible to grow crops in the cold climates where they live. The Inuit eat seals, walruses, polar bears, birds, fish, and other Arctic animals. The traditional Inuit diet also includes some plants that grow naturally in the Arctic, such as roots, berries, and seaweed. Surprisingly, even though the traditional diet is 50–75% fat and does not include a lot of vegetables, the Inuit who eat this diet are very healthy. Today, most Inuit eat a combination of a traditional and a more modern diet because they have access to a variety of food in grocery stores.

1. How is a traditional Inuit diet different from your diet?

_____

2. What shaped the traditional Inuit diet?

_____

3. How has a typical Inuit diet changed in recent years?

_____

C The words in **bold** below are used in the video. Read the sentences. Then match the correct form of each word to its definition.

> Antarctica is one of the world's most **remote** places.
>
> Not many plants and animals can **survive** in places with extreme climates.
>
> **Hunting** seals and polar bears for food is part of the Inuit's traditional **lifestyle**.

1. _____ (n) way of living

2. _____ (v) to kill animals for food

3. _____ (adj) far away from everything

4. _____ (v) to continue to live even in difficult situations

WHILE VIEWING

A ▶ Watch the video. What was Matthieu Paley's main goal in Greenland? Circle the most suitable answer.

a. to show the role that food plays in the Inuit culture

b. to show how the Inuit diet is affected by modern lifestyles

c. to learn about the effect fast food is having on the traditional Inuit diet

B ▶ Watch the video again. Put the events of Paley's experience in order (1–6).

_____ a. arrived in Isortoq

_____ b. spotted a seal's head in the ocean

_____ c. brought the seal back to the village

_____ d. went hunting with Magnus on a canoe

_____ e. went hunting with Bengt and Dina and caught a seal

_____ f. asked Dina if she could show him a real Arctic dish

AFTER VIEWING

A Which of Paley's Greenland photos do you remember best from the video? How would you describe it? Discuss your ideas with a partner.

_____

_____

B Note your answer to the question below. Then discuss with a partner.

Do you think Paley achieved his main goal? Why or why not?

_____

_____

Reading 2

PREPARING TO READ

A The words in **blue** below are used in the reading passage on pages 92–93. Complete each sentence with the correct word.

BUILDING VOCABULARY

A **dish** is a kind of meal or recipe.

If something is **popular**, a lot of people like it.

When you **argue** with someone, you disagree with them.

A **recipe** is a set of instructions for making a type of food.

When you **hope** to do something, you want and expect to do it.

If you **respect** someone, you like them for their ability or knowledge.

An **ingredient** is one of the things that you use to make a particular dish or meal.

A **variety** is a group of things of a particular type that are all different in some way.

1. I _____ my grandfather for his patience and kindness.

2. Salt is an important _____. Cooks use it in almost every kind of _____.

3. Some restaurants have secret _____ for making their food.

4. People often _____ on social media when they don't agree on a topic.

5. You can learn to cook a(n) _____ of dishes from food blogs.

6. If you _____ to create a(n) _____ blog, you should write about things that a lot of people are interested in.

B Discuss these questions with a partner.

USING VOCABULARY

1. Have you ever **argued** with people online?

2. Do you know any trends that are **popular** online now?

C Why do you think people read food blogs? List three reasons. Then share your ideas with a partner.

BRAINSTORMING

1. _____

2. _____

3. _____

D The reading on page 92 is an interview with food blogger Sasha Martin. Look at the title of the reading. What do you think Martin writes about in her blog? Check your ideas as you read the passage.

PREDICTING

COOKING THE WORLD

🎧 10

A Award-winning food writer Sasha Martin started her popular *Global Table Adventure* blog in 2010. Her plan was simple: to prepare a meal from every country in the world. Over the next four years, she cooked over 650 dishes from 195 countries. In this interview, Martin describes her experience of cooking the world.

Was "cooking the world" a way to travel without leaving home?

B That's right. I think the idea that exploration is for everyone is really important. There are so many people who dream of travel. But I think that you really can go on adventures without leaving home.

C With food, if you have the right ingredients, you can create the flavor of another place. It's like armchair travel, but it's faster and easier. I call it "stovetop travel."

What did you hope to teach your daughter by cooking the world?

D I wanted her to feel that she had a place in the world where she belonged. But I also feel it's important for children to grow up knowing people from other countries—their global neighbors.

E I call them neighbors because the world is so small now. I remember going on Facebook in its early days. I noticed there were people from different parts of the world commenting on posts, even arguing with each other. I feel that in that environment, young people need to be able to respect and understand each other.

So food is a great way to create that common ground?

F Yes. I wanted to share recipes that were bridges to other cultures. A lot of celebrity TV chefs tend to choose the most shocking recipes. But I think you need a bridge first. Then people won't put up a wall in their mind about that culture. They won't just think, "Gross[1]! Those people eat such weird[2] things!"

[1] gross: very unpleasant, disgusting   [2] weird: strange

One of Sasha Martin's recipes—Peruvian quinoa salad with olives and avocado

Sasha Martin and her daughter Ava

THE RISE OF THE FOOD BLOGGER

In July 1997, there was only one food blog on the Internet; today there are over two million. That first blog, *Chowhound*, was an online discussion board for sharing ideas about eating in New York. Today, food bloggers cover a wide **variety** of topics. Some examples:

- When Adam Roberts was in law school, he needed a break from studying. He decided to teach himself how to cook. Roberts started a blog to keep a record of his learning adventure and share it with other people. Eventually, his blog *The Amateur Gourmet* led to a new career in cooking.

- In May of 2012, two friends wanted to make each other laugh, so they created a blog for sharing pictures of ugly food. Other people began to send in their own photos of weird-looking food. By 2014, *Someone Ate This* was one of the Internet's most popular food blogs.

- A history student named Anje decided to share her love for history and cooking. On her websites, *Kitchen Historic* and *Food Roots*, readers can find dishes from the 13th century all the way to the 1980s.

UNDERSTANDING THE READING

UNDERSTANDING
MAIN IDEAS

A Check (✓) the three sentences that best describe Martin's blog and ideas.

☐ 1. Martin's blog provides a way to travel around the world without leaving home.

☐ 2. Martin's blog provides travel tips for making a journey around the world.

☐ 3. Martin thinks it's important for children to learn about other cultures.

☐ 4. Martin believes that food creates cultural connections.

☐ 5. Martin likes to include strange or unusual recipes on her blog.

UNDERSTANDING
DETAILS

B Why did each blogger create their food blog? Match each blogger to a reason or reasons (a–g).

a. to make each other laugh
b. to explore recipes from a long time ago
c. to go on adventures without leaving home
d. to help young people learn to respect each other
e. to share a learning experience with people
f. to share information about food in a particular city
g. to teach her daughter and readers about other cultures

1. Sasha Martin _____

2. the creators of _____
    Chowhound

3. Adam Roberts _____

4. Anje _____

5. the creators of _____
    Someone Ate This

UNDERSTANDING
PRONOUN
REFERENCE

C Underline the pronouns in these sentences. Then draw an arrow to the noun that each pronoun refers to.

1. When Adam Roberts was in law school, he needed a break from studying.

2. Roberts started a food blog and shared it with other people.

3. In May of 2012, two friends wanted to make each other laugh, so they created a blog for sharing pictures of ugly food.

CRITICAL THINKING:
JUSTIFYING
YOUR OPINION

D How much would you like to read each blog? Rate each one (1–3), and give a reason for your choice.

1 = I'm not interested in it.   ⟶   3 = I would really like to read it.

Global Table Adventure	1 2 3	_____
Chowhound	1 2 3	_____
The Amateur Gourmet	1 2 3	_____
Someone Ate This	1 2 3	_____
Kitchen Historic / Food Roots	1 2 3	_____

Writing

EXPLORING WRITTEN ENGLISH

A Read the sentences below. Check (✓) the three sentences that give reasons. Then underline a word or phrase in each one that connects the reason and the result.

NOTICING

- ☐ 1. He went on a journey to explore how our environment affects the food we eat.
- ☐ 2. Sasha Martin started the popular *Global Table Adventure* blog in 2010.
- ☐ 3. I call them neighbors because the world is so small now.
- ☐ 4. It looks like tiny asparagus and has a bitter taste.
- ☐ 5. In May of 2012, two friends wanted to make each other laugh, so they created a blog for sharing pictures of ugly food.

LANGUAGE FOR WRITING Giving Reasons

Here are some words and phrases you can use to give reasons.

> Adam Roberts started a food blog **because** he needed a break from school.
> Anje loves history and food, **so** she started a food blog.
> **One reason** (that) people start a blog is that they want to share their experiences.
> **Another reason** is (that) they want to improve their writing skills.
> Some people start blogs **to** tell their friends about their daily lives.

Notes:

- The reason comes before *so*, and the result follows it. A comma separates the two clauses.

- When an infinitive (*to* + base verb) is used to give a reason, *because*, a subject, and a verb can be left out in the reason clause.

  > Some people start blogs **(because they want) to tell** their friends about their daily lives.

- You can switch the clauses in sentences with *because*. A comma separates the two clauses in this case:

  > **Because** he needed a break from school, Adam Roberts started a food blog.

◀ One of the recipes Sasha Martin made was the German dessert baumkuchen, or "tree cake." It was given this name because the many layers inside look like the rings of a tree.

B Complete the sentences with a word or phrase for giving reasons.

1. De Los Santos asked photographers to take food pictures _____ she thinks it's a good way to learn about other cultures.

2. _____ people read Sasha Martin's blog is to find recipes. _____ is that they want to visit faraway places without leaving home.

3. Matthieu Paley took pictures of his travels _____ show the world typical food scenes from the places he visited.

4. People sometimes want to share their experiences, _____ they post photos of the food they eat.

5. Some chefs start food blogs _____ they want to write cookbooks.

6. Travelers often want to learn about local foods, _____ they read food blogs before they travel.

C Combine the sentences using a suitable word or phrase to make one sentence. There is more than one correct answer for some pairs of sentences.

1. Many people travel. They want to try new dishes.

   _____

2. In my opinion, *101 Cookbooks* is the best food blog. The photos are beautiful. The recipes are easy to follow.

   _____

   _____

3. Smartphones have good cameras. It's easy to take beautiful food pictures on a trip.

   _____

   _____

4. Paley wanted to show people the typical Arctic diet. He took pictures of a seal hunt.

   _____

   _____

WRITING SKILL Paraphrasing Using Synonyms

Paraphrasing is expressing the meaning of something using different words. One way of paraphrasing is using synonyms—words with a similar meaning—to avoid repeating the same word.

*Many people enjoy taking **photos** of **food**, but De Los Santos wanted more than just **pictures** of pretty **dishes**. She was also looking for great **photography**, so she used certain criteria for choosing the **images**.*

D Match each word with the best synonym (a–k).

1. _____ emotions
2. _____ typical
3. _____ role
4. _____ believe
5. _____ photo
6. _____ post
7. _____ fun
8. _____ delicious
9. _____ beautiful
10. _____ boring
11. _____ food

a. tasty
b. feelings
c. upload
d. uninteresting
e. part
f. usual
g. pretty
h. dish
i. think
j. enjoyable
k. picture

E Read the pairs of sentences below. Paraphrase the underlined part in each pair using synonyms. You can use the words in exercise D, or other words that you know.

1. Sasha Martin cooked dishes from all over the world. She <u>cooked</u> <u>dishes</u> from 195 different countries.

_____

_____

2. When Martin was young, she believed that cooking could be fun. As an adult, she still <u>believes</u> that <u>cooking</u> is <u>fun</u>.

_____

_____

3. Martin posts photos of her food online. Readers can <u>post</u> their own <u>photos</u> in the comments section of Martin's blog.

_____

_____

4. People often post photos of delicious and beautiful food that they cook. Other readers enjoy looking at the <u>photos</u> of the <u>delicious</u> <u>food</u>.

_____

_____

F Write a second sentence to follow each sentence below. Include a synonym of at least one of the words.

1. Matthieu Paley enjoyed a typical Mediterranean family meal in Crete.

_____

_____

2. Some people read food blogs because they want to get ideas for recipes.

_____

_____

WRITING TASK

> **GOAL** You are going to write a paragraph on the following topic:
>
> Explain why you think people like to share pictures of food on social media or on blogs. Give three reasons.

BRAINSTORMING **A** Read the list of reasons that people share photos of food on social media or on blogs. With a partner, brainstorm for more reasons.

They want to …
- tell people about a great meal that they ate
- tell people that they're eating healthy food
- get cooking advice
- give food or restaurant reviews

- _____
- _____
- _____

PLANNING **B** Follow these steps to make notes for your paragraph. Don't worry about grammar or spelling. Don't write complete sentences.

Step 1 Decide whether you are going to write about the sharing of food on social media or on blogs. Write a topic sentence.

Step 2 Look at your brainstorming notes. Rank your reasons and choose the top three. Write them in the outline as your supporting ideas.

Step 3 Add at least one detail for each reason.

> **OUTLINE**
>
> **Topic sentence:** _____
>
> **Supporting Idea 1:** _____
>
> _____
>
> Detail: _____
>
> **Supporting Idea 2:** _____
>
> _____
>
> Detail: _____
>
> **Supporting Idea 3:** _____
>
> _____
>
> Detail: _____

FIRST DRAFT **C** Use the information in your outline to write a first draft of your paragraph.

REVISING PRACTICE

The drafts below are similar to the one you are going to write, but they are on a different topic:

Explain why you think people should try food from different cultures. Give three reasons.

What did the writer do in Draft 2 to improve the paragraph? Match the changes (a–d) to the highlighted parts.

a. added a detail for a supporting idea   b. used a synonym

c. deleted unrelated information   d. added a word or phrase that introduces a reason

Draft 1

I believe that it is important for people to try food from different cultures. They will learn about other countries. When they research recipes for food from other countries and try new ingredients, they will discover new things about those places. It's important to follow a recipe when you are cooking something new. Also, people should try foreign foods because they can experience a country without actually going there. It can be expensive to travel to a foreign country, but it's easy and inexpensive to try a dish from that country. Finally, I think people should try food from other cultures to make cooking and eating more enjoyable.

Draft 2

I believe that it is important for people to try food from different cultures. One reason is that they will learn about other countries. When they research recipes for food from other countries and try new ingredients, they will discover new things about those places. Also, people should try foreign foods because they can experience a country without actually going there. It can be expensive to travel to a foreign country, but it's easy and inexpensive to try a dish from that place. Finally, I think people should try food from other cultures to make cooking and eating more enjoyable. Eating the same dishes all the time is boring, and trying different types of food can be an adventure.

D Now use the questions below to revise your paragraph.

    ☐ Did you use suitable words and phrases to introduce reasons?

    ☐ Did you include a detail for each supporting idea?

    ☐ Did you use synonyms to avoid repetition?

    ☐ Do all your sentences relate to the main idea?

REVISED DRAFT

EDITING PRACTICE

Read the information below.

In sentences with words and phrases that show reasons, remember:
- that the reason comes before *so*, and the result comes after it.
- that in sentences with *so*, a comma separates the two clauses.
- to separate the two clauses with a comma when you begin a sentence with *because*.
- that in an infinitive, the base form of the verb always follows *to*.

Correct one mistake with language for introducing reasons in each of the sentences (1–6).

1. Some people want to share their good eating habits so they post pictures of their meals on social media.

2. I think people post pictures of the food they make to sharing their hobby with their friends.

3. Food blogger Clotilde Dusoulier quit her job so she wanted to become a full-time food writer.

4. Because they want to make some money some food bloggers have ads on their sites.

5. People read food blogs, because they need ideas for things to make for dinner.

6. Some people post pictures of their food to tells people about new restaurants in town.

FINAL DRAFT **E** Follow these steps to write a final draft.

1. Check your revised draft for mistakes with language for introducing reasons.

2. Now use the checklist on page 218 to write a final draft. Make any other necessary changes.

UNIT REVIEW
Answer the following questions.

1. What is one thing you learned in this unit about food in a different culture?

_____

_____

_____

2. What are two words or phrases you can use to introduce a reason?

_____

_____

3. Do you remember the meanings of these words? Check (✓) the ones you know. Look back at the unit and review the ones you don't know.

Reading 1:

☐ culture ᴬᵂᴸ   ☐ fresh   ☐ fried
☐ offer   ☐ pick   ☐ prepare
☐ share   ☐ taste   ☐ type
☐ typical

Reading 2:

☐ argue   ☐ dish   ☐ hope
☐ ingredient   ☐ popular   ☐ recipe
☐ respect   ☐ variety

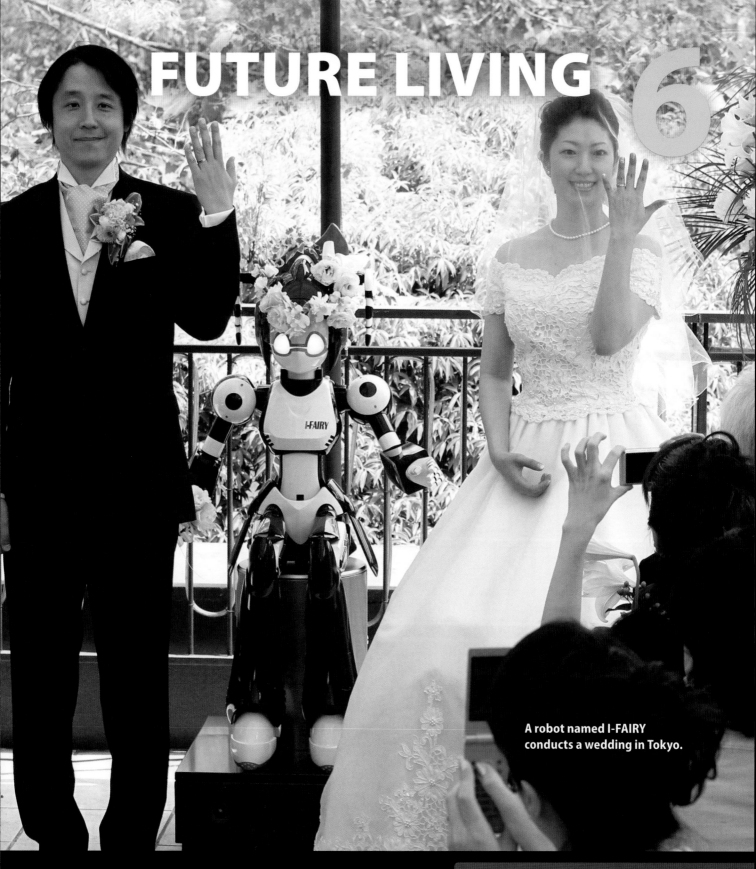

FUTURE LIVING 6

A robot named I-FAIRY
conducts a wedding in Tokyo.

THINK AND DISCUSS

1 How do you think life will be different 50 years from now? How about in 100 years?
2 Do you think we will live on other planets someday? Why or why not?

EXPLORE THE THEME

A Look at the information on these pages and answer the questions.

1. Which future technology or feature do you think is most useful?

2. Are any of these happening already? Can you give an example?

B Match the words in blue to their definitions.

_____ (v) to change in order to deal with something

_____ (n) scientific knowledge or skill

_____ (v) to say what will happen in the future

THE CITY OF THE FUTURE

What will cities be like in the future? Experts predict that technology will change the design of our cities and the way we live.

Wearable technology

People will wear devices that communicate with their surroundings. The devices will provide useful information as they move around the city.

Underground travel

More people will ride bicycles and other forms of travel that don't pollute the environment. In busy areas, they will ride underground in special bicycle lanes to avoid traffic.

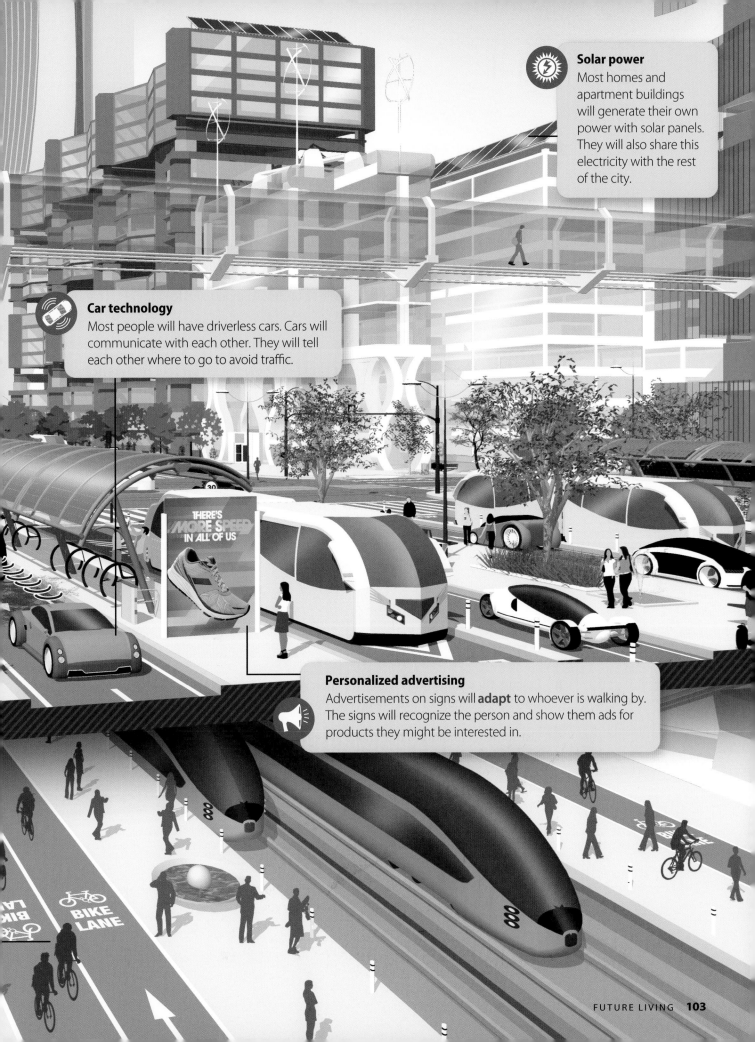

Solar power
Most homes and apartment buildings will generate their own power with solar panels. They will also share this electricity with the rest of the city.

Car technology
Most people will have driverless cars. Cars will communicate with each other. They will tell each other where to go to avoid traffic.

THERE'S **MORE SPEED** IN ALL OF US

Personalized advertising
Advertisements on signs will **adapt** to whoever is walking by. The signs will recognize the person and show them ads for products they might be interested in.

BIKE LANE

Reading 1

PREPARING TO READ

BUILDING
VOCABULARY

A The words in **blue** below are used in the reading passage on pages 105–106. Read the sentences. Then match the correct form of each word to its definition.

> Most companies have their own computer **networks**. These networks **link** computers to each other.
>
> Pepper is a **sociable** robot that's able to understand people's feelings and change the way it communicates with them.
>
> You can **store** information like phone numbers and addresses on your smartphone.
>
> Online movie and TV sites **suggest** films and shows based on your **preferences** and what you usually watch.
>
> Driverless cars are an example of **intelligent** technology. They can take you where you want to go, avoid traffic, and park themselves.

1. _____ (v) to connect

2. _____ (adj) friendly to people

3. _____ (n) what you like or don't like

4. _____ (v) to give people ideas about what they should do

5. _____ (adj) able to understand and learn things

6. _____ (n) a system of connected communication lines

7. _____ (v) to keep somewhere for future use

USING
VOCABULARY

B Discuss these questions with a partner: What are some examples of **intelligent** devices you know or use? What can they do?

BRAINSTORMING

C List some technologies that make life easier or more fun today than in the past.

Technologies That Make Life Easier	Technologies That Make Life More Fun
high-speed trains	3-D movies

PREDICTING

D Skim the reading passage on pages 105–106 quickly. Check (✓) the topics that the passage covers. Then check your answers as you read.

☐ 1. cars that drive themselves

☐ 2. things in the home that send information to one another

☐ 3. computers that control the house

☐ 4. robots that are like people

In the future, new technology will change many of our daily routines.

HOW WILL WE LIVE?

🎧 11

A   Picture this: You wake up in the morning. A soft light turns on in your room. You go into the bathroom and the shower starts. The water is the perfect temperature. After your shower, you go into the kitchen. Your favorite breakfast is already cooked, and it's on the table, ready to eat. Now it's time to go to work. It's a rainy day. You live alone, but you find that your umbrella and hat are already by the door. How is all this possible? Welcome to your future life!

APPLIANCES THAT TALK

B   Technology will allow homes in the future to be "smart." Appliances will communicate with each other—and with you. Your stove, for instance, will tell you when your food is cooked and ready to eat. Refrigerators will suggest recipes based on food items you already have.

C   The technology is possible because of tiny information-storing devices called RFID[1] chips. People already use them to keep track of pets and farm animals. Future RFID chips will store information about all the items in your cabinets.[2] For example, they will record the date that you bought each item. Other devices will "read" this information using radio waves. When you need more food, your cabinets will tell you to buy it.

[1] RFID stands for "radio-frequency identification."
[2] A cabinet is a type of cupboard used for storing medicine, drinks, and other items.

HOUSES THAT THINK

D Are you tired of the color or pattern of your walls? In a smart home, you won't have to repaint them. The walls will actually be digital screens, like computer or TV screens. The technology is called OLED,[3] and it's here already. OLEDs are tiny devices that use electricity to light things. You can find the same technology in today's thin TV screens. OLED walls can become clear, like windows, or display colors and patterns, like walls.

E A computer **network** will **link** these walls with everything else in your house. This **intelligent** technology works like a computer "brain" that controls your entire house. It will also **adapt** to your **preferences**. Your house can learn about your likes and dislikes. It will then use that knowledge to control the environment. For example, it will set the heat in the house to your favorite temperature. It will turn on the shower at the right heat. It will also darken the windows at night and lighten them when it's time to wake up.

ROBOTS THAT FEEL?

F But how about your cooked breakfast, and the umbrella and hat you found by the door? For those, you can thank your robot helper. Futurologists **predict** that many homes will have robots in the future. Robots already do many things, such as building cars and vacuuming floors. But scientists today are starting to build friendlier, more intelligent robots—ones that people will feel more comfortable having around in the house.

G **Sociable** robots will be able to show feelings with their faces, just like humans. They will smile and frown, make eye contact, and speak. These robots will do work around the house, such as cooking and cleaning. They will even take care of children and the elderly.

H How soon will this smart home be a reality? There's a good chance it will be a part of your life in the next 10 years, perhaps sooner. Much of the technology is already here.

[3]**OLED** stands for "organic light-emitting diode."

Robots like **ASIMO** can already do many things that people do.

UNDERSTANDING THE READING

A Match each main idea below to a paragraph (A–H) from the reading. Three paragraphs are extra.

UNDERSTANDING MAIN IDEAS

_____ 1. An intelligent electronic system will control an entire house.

_____ 2. Information-storing technology will allow parts of the house to communicate with us.

_____ 3. Digital technology will allow us to change the design of our homes.

_____ 4. Intelligent homes may be a part of our everyday life within 10 years.

_____ 5. Robots that act like humans will do housework and take care of people.

B According to the passage, is each statement below true? Or is it not mentioned? Circle T for *true*, F for *false*, or NG for *not given*.

UNDERSTANDING DETAILS

Appliances That Talk

1. Appliances will make personalized suggestions using information they collect. **T   F   NG**

2. RFID is a type of smart refrigerator that can recommend recipes. **T   F   NG**

Houses That Think

3. Future technology will make houses safer from natural disasters. **T   F   NG**

4. Houses will be able to change the temperature of the room based on your preferences. **T   F   NG**

Robots That Feel?

5. Robots will have human-like expressions. **T   F   NG**

6. Sociable robots will help us in our homes. **T   F   NG**

> **CRITICAL THINKING**   **Inferring** a writer's **attitude** means thinking about how they feel about the subject. Ask yourself: Is the author generally positive or negative? What clues indicate the author's attitude?

C Work with a partner. First, circle a word to complete the sentence below. Then find an example from the passage that supports your answer.

CRITICAL THINKING: INFERRING ATTITUDE

The author of the reading passage seems **positive** / **negative** about life in the future.

According to the author, _____

_____

_____

D Discuss these questions with a partner.

CRITICAL THINKING: APPLYING

1. Which future technologies in the reading would you like to have in your home?

2. Can you think of any other household technologies that would be useful?

DEVELOPING READING SKILLS

> **READING SKILL** Identifying Examples
>
> Writers often give examples to support their ideas. Here are some common words or phrases they use. Note the position of the commas.
>
> *Someday, your refrigerator will be able to communicate with you.* **For example**, *it will suggest recipes based on food you already have.*
>
> *People use RFID chips today for many things,* **such as** *keeping track of pets and farm animals.*
>
> *In the future, robots will be more like humans.* **For instance**, *they will smile, frown, make eye contact, and speak.*

IDENTIFYING
EXAMPLES

A Circle the words and phrases that introduce examples in the following paragraph about Wakamaru. Then underline the examples.

Engineers in Japan built a sociable robot named Wakamaru. They designed Wakamaru to help and serve people in a friendly, caring, and intelligent way. For instance, Wakamaru can recognize faces, use gestures, and understand 10,000 Japanese words. It is able to talk to people about a variety of topics, such as the weather and the news. Wakamaru can do many tasks for a family. For example, at night, it moves quietly around the house, but it can wake family members up if there is any trouble. During the day, Wakamaru can send them email and text messages.

IDENTIFYING
EXAMPLES

B Match each example (a–e) to a sentence or sentence part (1–5).

____ 1. Mobile technology has changed the way we shop.

____ 2. I think intelligent robots can help with dangerous tasks,

____ 3. Everyday activities,

____ 4. Some people are worried about the safety of using smart technology.

____ 5. There are many ways we can reduce the number of cars on the road.

a. such as looking for people after a natural disaster.

b. Hackers, for instance, could steal personal information stored on our phones.

c. For example, we could cycle to work instead of driving.

d. such as cleaning and cooking, could be made more convenient with intelligent technology.

e. For example, we can buy things through an app on our smartphone.

INTRODUCING
EXAMPLES

C Add an example or examples to each sentence. Use a suitable phrase to introduce the example(s).

1. I think living in a smart home would make life more convenient. _____

_____

2. I would like to live with a robot. I would ask it to do many things, _____

_____

Video

NASA's Curiosity Rover explores Mars to help scientists study the planet.

LIVING ON MARS

BEFORE VIEWING

A Look at the photo and the title of the video. What do you think are some of the challenges of living on Mars? Discuss with a partner.

PREDICTING

B Read the information about Mars. Then note the three reasons why Mars may be a suitable planet for people to live on.

LEARNING ABOUT THE TOPIC

Of all the planets near Earth, Mars is the best possible option for humans to live on. There are many reasons why Mars is our first choice. First of all, the length of a day on Mars is more similar to the length of a day on Earth than any other planet in our solar system. A day on Mars lasts about 24 hours, but a day on Venus lasts about 243 Earth days. In addition, Mars gets enough light from the sun. This means we can use solar panels for power. Finally, even though Mars is much colder than Earth, its temperature is closer than other planets to Earth's temperature. Venus, for instance, is much too hot—its average temperature is over 400 degrees Celsius.

1. _____

2. _____

3. _____

C The words in **bold** below are used in the video. Read the paragraph. Then match the correct form of each word to its definition.

There have been dozens of **missions** to Mars during the past 30 years, but no humans have ever gone there. Some scientists have **ambitious** plans to **colonize** Mars. However, we have to make changes to Mars's **atmosphere** before we can live there. For example, we need to make it warmer, and we have to add oxygen (O_2) into the air.

1. _____ (n) the air space above a planet

2. _____ (v) to go to a place, live in it, and control it

3. _____ (n) an important job that usually involves travel

4. _____ (adj) very difficult or challenging to do

WHILE VIEWING

A ▶ Watch the video. Circle the name of the correct scientist.

1. **Dr. McKay / Dr. Zubrin** is disappointed that humans haven't been to Mars yet.

2. **Dr. McKay / Dr. Zubrin** is doing research to prepare for a mission to Mars.

3. **Dr. McKay / Dr. Zubrin** studies how we can change the atmosphere on Mars.

B ▶ Watch the video again. Why do the scientists say we will be successful in colonizing Mars? Check (✓) the reasons mentioned in the video.

☐ 1. Countries around the world are now working together on a mission to Mars.

☐ 2. We are doing research in places that have similar conditions to Mars.

☐ 3. We have successfully grown a plant on Mars.

☐ 4. We know how to warm the atmosphere on Mars.

☐ 5. We know a way to create oxygen on Mars.

AFTER VIEWING

A Discuss with a partner: Do you think it's a good idea for people to go to Mars? Why or why not?

☐ Yes, I do.   ☐ I'm not sure.   ☐ Definitely not.

Reason:

_____

B Which technologies in the reading on pages 105–106 might be useful for living on Mars? Why? Note your ideas and discuss with a partner.

_____

_____

_____

Reading 2

PREPARING TO READ

A The words in **blue** below are used in the reading passage on pages 112–113. Read the paragraph. Then match the correct form of each word to its definition.

BUILDING VOCABULARY

We know that it is very cold on Mars. Scientists recorded the temperature in several places on the planet. They took these temperatures to find out the **average** temperature on Mars, which is minus 60 degrees Celsius. Because the temperature is so low, there is no **liquid** on Mars—only ice. Carbon dioxide (CO_2) is **trapped** in this ice—it cannot get out. However, heat can melt the ice and turn it into water. This can **release** the carbon dioxide into the atmosphere. When the **level** of carbon dioxide increases in the atmosphere, Mars will become warmer.

1. _____ (v) to stop holding; to let go

2. _____ (adj) the middle of two extremes

3. _____ (v) to hold and keep from moving

4. _____ (n) a substance that flows freely, such as water or oil

5. _____ (n) a point on a scale, usually showing the amount of something

B Complete the sentences below using the words in the box. Use your dictionary to help you with the meanings of the words.

BUILDING VOCABULARY

| environment   plants   lack |

1. _____ need sun and water to grow.

2. Earth's _____ is very suitable for life.

3. The _____ of oxygen on high mountains makes it difficult to breathe.

C Discuss these questions with a partner.

USING VOCABULARY

1. What kind of **plants** grow well in your area?

2. What kind of **environment** is best for growing plants?

D Read the title of the reading passage and look at the picture on pages 112–113. What do you think the passage is about? Then check your answer as you read.

PREDICTING

a. the technology we will use to travel to Mars and other planets

b. what an average day on Mars will be like for people in the future

c. how we can make Mars a place where people can live

AT HOME ON MARS

△ 12

A   Will humans someday live and work on Mars? Many scientists think so. In fact, they are already working on plans to turn Mars into a new Earth.

B   Humans need three basic things to live: water to drink, air to breathe, and food to eat. Because of the lack of these necessities, it isn't possible to live on Mars right now. For one thing, there is not enough oxygen. There is also no liquid water—just some ice. So how can we make Mars habitable?[1] The answer, scientists suggest, is a process called *terraforming*.

C   Terraforming means changing the environment of a planet so that it is similar to Earth's. On Mars, the average temperature is about minus 60 degrees Celsius. So one goal of terraforming Mars is to warm it up. Most scientists agree that Earth is becoming warmer due to increased levels of greenhouse gases in our atmosphere. We might be able to create similar conditions on Mars.

D   One solution is to build factories on Mars that release greenhouse gases. The gases will change the Martian atmosphere, resulting in warmer temperatures. Mars's polar regions will begin to melt, releasing more carbon dioxide trapped inside the ice. Rain will eventually fall. It may then be possible to grow plants outdoors for food. The plants will add oxygen to the air, making human colonies on Mars a real possibility.

[1] If a place is **habitable,** you can live there.

TURNING THE RED PLANET GREEN

1 FIRST VISITS

Terraforming Mars will probably be a thousand-year project, starting with several survey missions. The flight to Mars will take 6 months, but the entire mission might last more than 18 months.

2 HOMES ON MARS

Each new mission will build more habitation modules—places to live. These will allow future visitors to spend more time on Mars and learn more about living on the planet.

3 GLOBAL WARMING

Factories on Mars will release carbon dioxide into the atmosphere, warming the planet and allowing water to flow.

4 LIFE UNDER DOMES

Enormous domes will provide climate-controlled living spaces, first for plants and later for humans. It will take centuries to improve the rocky surface so that people can grow plants.

5 POWERING THE PLANET

Nuclear power[2] and wind turbines[3] are two current technologies that we might be able to use on Mars.

6 DON'T FORGET YOUR MASK

Even 1,000 years from now, there may not be enough oxygen for humans to breathe, so people on Mars may still need to use special breathing equipment.

[2]**Nuclear power** comes from the energy that is released when the central parts of atoms are split or combined.
[3]**Wind turbines** are engines with blades. They produce power when wind spins the blades.

UNDERSTANDING THE READING

UNDERSTANDING
MAIN IDEAS

A Read the first sentence of a summary of paragraphs A–D. Check (✓) three other sentences to complete the summary.

If we want to live on Mars someday, we will have to change it so it is similar to Earth.

☐ 1. Wind turbines can produce power using wind energy.

☐ 2. We will need to increase the average temperature of Mars.

☐ 3. A huge amount of greenhouse gases is making Earth's atmosphere warmer.

☐ 4. Releasing greenhouse gases on Mars will help create a suitable environment.

☐ 5. Changing Mars will be a long process, but scientists think we will live there someday.

SEQUENCING

B How do scientists plan to terraform Mars? Use information from pages 112–113 to complete the timeline.

a. Factories on Mars's surface produce carbon dioxide.

b. Rain begins to fall and water flows.

c. Early visitors build living spaces.

d. Plants can grow on Mars's surface.

e. The temperature on Mars begins to rise.

f. Ice in polar regions starts to melt.

first survey mission ⟶ **humans colonize Mars**

IDENTIFYING
PROBLEMS AND
SOLUTIONS

C Write a short answer to each question.

1. How might human visitors get their power on Mars?

_____

_____

2. What will still be a problem for humans on Mars 1,000 years from now?

_____

_____

CRITICAL THINKING:
JUSTIFYING
YOUR OPINION

D Some companies are planning a trip to Mars and are looking for people to join them. Would you join a mission to Mars? Check your answer below. Then write two sentences to explain your reasons.

☐ Yes, I'd love to.   ☐ I'm not sure.   ☐ Definitely not.

Reasons:

1. _____

2. _____

Writing

EXPLORING WRITTEN ENGLISH

A Read the sentences below. Check (✓) the ones where the underlined part is …

1. **an additional idea:**

☐ a. Humans need three basic things to live: water to drink, air to breathe, and <u>food to eat</u>.

☐ b. There will be <u>many difficulties in terraforming Mars</u>.

2. **a contrasting idea:**

☐ a. A computer network will link these walls with <u>everything else in your house</u>.

☐ b. Robots already do many things such as building cars and vacuuming floors. But <u>scientists today are starting to build friendlier, more intelligent robots</u>.

3. **a result:**

☐ a. Some scientists believe that <u>it's possible to colonize Mars in the future</u>.

☐ b. Even 1,000 years from now, there may still not be enough oxygen for humans to breathe, so <u>people on Mars may still need to use special breathing equipment</u>.

LANGUAGE FOR WRITING Using *And*, *But*, and *So*

You can use the conjunctions *and*, *but*, and *so* to connect information in sentences.

And introduces an additional idea …

• to connect words: *People will visit <u>Mars</u> **and** <u>Venus</u>.*

• to connect phrases: *People will <u>visit Mars</u> **and** <u>build habitation modules</u>.*

• to connect clauses: <u>*People will visit Mars*</u>, ***and*** <u>*they will build habitation modules*</u>.

But introduces a contrasting idea …

• to connect words: *It's <u>hot</u> **but** <u>habitable</u>.*

• to connect phrases: *People will live <u>on Mars</u> **but** <u>not on Venus</u>.*

• to connect clauses: <u>*People will live on Mars*</u>, ***but*** <u>*they won't live on Venus*</u>.

So introduces results …

• to connect clauses: <u>*It's very cold on Mars*</u>, ***so*** <u>*we will need to warm it up*</u>.

Remember:

• to use a comma when you connect clauses.

• when you use *and* and *but*, repeated subjects and auxiliary verbs in the second clause can be removed:

<u>*People*</u> <u>*will*</u> *live on Mars.* <u>*People*</u> <u>*will*</u> *work on Mars.*

    subject   auxiliary verb   subject   auxiliary verb

*People will live **and** work on Mars.*

B Complete the sentences with *and*, *but*, or *so*.

1. Missions to Mars are expensive, _____ we probably won't send people there for many years.

2. Scientists have sent robots to the moon _____ to Mars.

3. Smart technology can help us do things more quickly _____ efficiently.

4. Scientists have an idea for warming up Mars, _____ it will take a long time before the planet is suitable for humans to live on.

5. There is no liquid water on Mars, _____ plants cannot grow there.

6. NASA wanted to send people to Mars 30 years ago, _____ the government didn't have enough money.

7. People have already been to the moon, _____ they haven't been to Mars.

8. Travel to Mars is dangerous, _____ we will send robots instead.

C Combine the sentences using *and*, *but*, or *so*. Leave out the pronoun and auxiliary verb where possible.

Example: Robots can vacuum houses. They can build cars.

      Robots can vacuum houses and build cars.

1. PR2—a robot—can take care of elderly people. It can deliver mail.

    _____

2. PR2 cooks. It doesn't communicate.

    _____

3. Wakamaru knows 10,000 Japanese words. It is able to communicate with people.

    _____

4. There is not enough oxygen on Mars. Humans cannot breathe there.

    _____

D Work with a partner. Think of an item that will be different in the future. Think about what it will look like and how it will work. Note your ideas in the chart. Then write a sentence about the item using *and*, *but*, or *so*.

Object	What It Will Look Like / How It Will Work

_____

_____

WRITING SKILL Using Pronouns to Avoid Repetition

As you learned in Unit 5, pronouns usually refer to nouns that appear earlier in a text. You can use pronouns to avoid repetition.

Example: *Robots will do many things around the house. For example, robots will clean the house and prepare food.*

*Robots will do many things around the house. For example, **they** will clean the house and prepare food.*

Try not to use a pronoun that can refer to more than one thing in a sentence, as this can be confusing. For example, in the sentence "Robots will work with people, and they will become more efficient," the word "they" could refer to "robots" or "people."

E Draw a line through the repeated nouns in the sentences and replace them with suitable pronouns.

USING PRONOUNS

1. RFID chips will keep track of the food in your cabinets, and RFID chips will tell you when it's time to go to the store.

2. People on survey missions to Mars will build domes and live in the domes.

3. People will terraform Mars and make Mars more like Earth.

4. Even after a thousand years, people won't be able to breathe on Mars, so people will have to use breathing equipment.

5. Mars doesn't have any oxygen, but plants will slowly add oxygen to the atmosphere over many years.

F Read the sentences below. What does each underlined pronoun refer to? Use a word or phrase from the box. The words can be used more than once.

IDENTIFYING PRONOUN REFERENCE

people	the robots	the domes	the color

1. Sociable robots will communicate with people. <u>They</u> will speak to <u>them</u> and make eye contact with them.

   they = _____   them = _____

2. People will build domes on Mars. They will live and grow plants in <u>them</u>.

   them = _____

3. People will use OLED screens to change the color of their walls. If they don't like <u>it</u>, they will just push a button and change it.

   it = _____

4. In the future, people will wear devices that communicate with their surroundings. The devices will provide useful information as <u>they</u> walk around the city.

   they = _____

WRITING TASK

> **GOAL** You are going to write a paragraph on the following topic:
> What will a typical day be like in 2050?

BRAINSTORMING **A** Imagine a typical day in 2050. What will it be like? Brainstorm some ideas about your typical day in the future. Use these categories or your own ideas.

Study: _____

Work: _____

Travel: _____

Entertainment: _____

Other things: _____

PLANNING **B** Follow these steps to make notes for your paragraph. Don't worry about grammar or spelling. Don't write complete sentences.

Step 1 Choose three categories you want to write about (e.g., your home, work, and travel). Note them as your supporting ideas in the outline.

Step 2 Write a topic sentence for your paragraph.

Step 3 Use your brainstorming notes above to add at least one detail for each category.

OUTLINE

Topic sentence: *On a typical day in 2050,* _____

_____

Supporting Idea 1: _____

_____

Details: _____

_____

Supporting Idea 2: _____

_____

Details: _____

_____

Supporting Idea 3: _____

_____

Details: _____

_____

FIRST DRAFT **C** Use the information in your outline to write a first draft of your paragraph.

REVISING PRACTICE

The drafts below are similar to the one you are going to write, but they are on a different topic:

What will the typical home be like in 2050?

What did the writer do in Draft 2 to improve the paragraph? Match the changes (a–d) to the highlighted parts.

a. added an example to expand on a supporting idea
b. used a pronoun to avoid repetition
c. added a phrase to introduce an example
d. connected sentences with *and*, *but*, or *so*

Draft 1

A typical home in 2050 will be very different from a home of today. First of all, smart appliances will make our lives easier. Refrigerators will know how much food we have, so refrigerators will tell us when we need to go shopping. In addition, computers will control systems in the house. Finally, most homes will have robots that will help around the house. They will do important jobs, such as cleaning and cooking. They will also take care of people.

Draft 2

A typical home in 2050 will be very different from a home of today. First of all, smart appliances will make our lives easier. For example, refrigerators will know how much food we have, so they will tell us when we need to go shopping. In addition, computers will control systems in the house. For instance, computers will learn what we like and don't like, and control things around the house, such as lighting and temperature. Finally, most homes will have robots that will help around the house. They will do important jobs, such as cleaning, cooking, and taking care of people. ☐

D Now use the questions below to revise your paragraph.

REVISED DRAFT

☐ Did you include at least one detail for each supporting idea?

☐ Do all your sentences relate to the main idea?

☐ Did you use pronouns to avoid repetition?

☐ Did you include examples?

☐ Did you connect sentences with *and*, *but*, or *so* where suitable?

EDITING PRACTICE

Read the information below.

In sentences with *and*, *but*, or *so*, remember to:
- use *and* to introduce an additional idea, *but* to introduce a contrasting idea, and *so* to introduce a result.
- use a comma when you connect two clauses.
- leave out repeated subjects and auxiliary verbs when joining ideas using *and* or *but*.

Correct one mistake with *and*, *but*, or *so* in each of the sentences (1–7).

1. People will live on Mars someday, and it is too expensive to travel there now.

2. Mars is too cold for human visitors, but scientists will need to warm it up.

3. Robots will take care of children so do housework.

4. A trip to Mars sounds amazing, and I would not like to live there!

5. Smart appliances will buy food but cook dinner.

6. We might have flying cars in 2050, and there might be fewer cars on our roads.

7. In the future, you might have a language chip in your brain but you won't have to study foreign languages.

FINAL DRAFT **E** Follow these steps to write a final draft.

1. Check your revised draft for mistakes with *and*, *but*, or *so*.

2. Now use the checklist on page 218 to write a final draft. Make any other necessary changes.

UNIT REVIEW

Answer the following questions.

1. Which prediction for the future in this unit do you think is the most interesting? Why?

_____

_____

_____

2. What are some phrases that introduce an example?

_____

_____

_____

3. Do you remember the meanings of these words? Check (✔) the ones you know. Look back at the unit and review the ones you don't know.

Reading 1:

☐ adapt AWL   ☐ intelligent AWL   ☐ link AWL
☐ network AWL   ☐ predict AWL   ☐ preference
☐ sociable   ☐ store   ☐ suggest
☐ technology AWL

Reading 2:

☐ average   ☐ environment AWL   ☐ lack
☐ level   ☐ liquid   ☐ plant
☐ release AWL   ☐ trap

EXPLORATION 7

A diver finds a cow's skull in an underwater cave in Yucatán, Mexico.

ACADEMIC SKILLS

READING	Identifying facts and speculations
WRITING	Introducing examples
GRAMMAR	Expressing interests and desires
CRITICAL THINKING	Understanding analogies

THINK AND DISCUSS

1 Do you know of any famous explorers? What do/did they do?
2 What places would you like to explore?

A Look at the information on these pages and answer the questions.

1. What is the Mariana Trench? What is special about it?

2. Who has successfully traveled to the bottom of the Mariana Trench alone?

B Match the words in blue to their definitions.

_____ (v) to be in a particular place

_____ (v) to go through something and know how it feels

_____ (adj) far down from the top or surface

240 meters

average U.S. navy submarine

1,500 meters

elephant seal

EXPLORING THE MARIANA TRENCH

Located in the Pacific Ocean about 300 kilometers off Guam, the Mariana Trench is the deepest place in the world. It is like a deep valley. The deepest point—Challenger Deep—is about 11 kilometers below the ocean surface.

In 2012, film director James Cameron became the first person to experience traveling alone to Challenger Deep. Traveling in a submarine—*Deepsea Challenger*—he explored the bottom for more than two hours, taking videos and collecting samples.

Ocean Surface

30 meters

scuba diver

1,000 meters

No sunlight beyond this point

1,000 meters

2,000 meters

sperm whale

2,000 meters

3,000 meters

3,800 meters

wreck of the RMS *Titanic*

4,000 meters

5,000 meters

MOUNT EVEREST

6,000 meters

7,000 meters

If Mount Everest were underwater, it would not reach the bottom of the trench.

8,000 meters

8,848 meters

9,000 meters

Deepsea Challenger

10,000 meters

10,898 meters

Challenger Deep

11,000 meters

Reading 1

PREPARING TO READ

BUILDING
VOCABULARY **A** The words in **blue** below are used in the reading passage on pages 125–126. Read the paragraph. Then match the correct form of each word to its definition.

Many archaeologists dream of being able to **discover** a lost city. In 2017, that dream became a reality for a team of archaeologists in Honduras. They were the first people to explore a remote **region** of the Central American rain forest. The team found the remains of a **massive** pyramid **hidden** in the jungle. It also identified more than 50 stone sculptures in the pyramid; many more objects may be buried **underground**. The **artifacts** are thought to be over a thousand years old, and belong to an **ancient** culture that disappeared long ago.

1. _____ (n) area

2. _____ (v) to find

3. _____ (adj) very old

4. _____ (adj) very large

5. _____ (adj) not easy to see

6. _____ (adj) below the surface of the Earth

7. _____ (n) an object that people made a long time ago

USING
VOCABULARY **B** Discuss these questions with a partner.

1. Are there any places in your city that are **underground**? What are they?

2. Which **region** of your country do you live in? Are there any other regions of your country you would like to visit?

PREDICTING **C** Look at the photo and the title of the reading passage on page 125. What kind of "secret cities" do you think are described in the passage? What do you think they were used for? Discuss your ideas with a partner.

_____

_____

I think the cities are probably …   *They might be used for … because …*

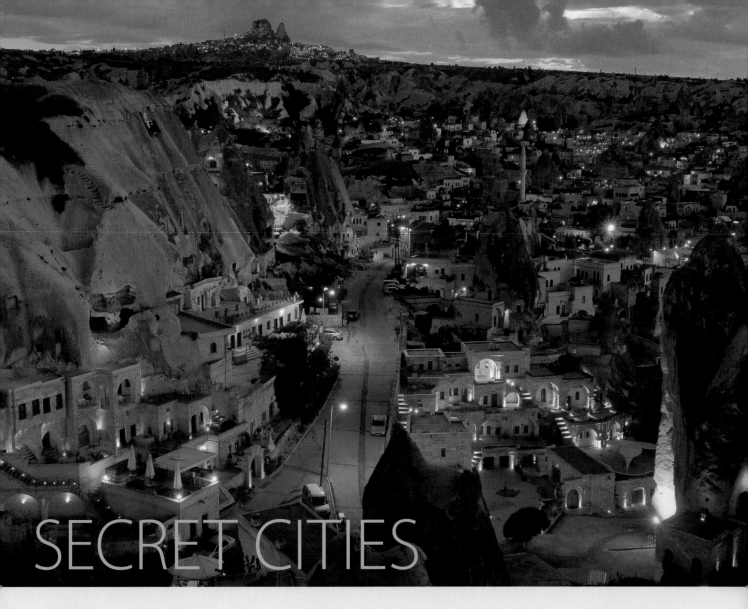

SECRET CITIES

🎧 13

A In 1963, a resident of the Cappadocia **region** of Turkey was doing some renovations[1] on his house. When he knocked down one of his walls, he was surprised to find a **hidden** room carved into the stone. He explored the room, and found that it led to an **underground** city—the city of Derinkuyu.

B The underground city is over 60 meters **deep**—deep enough for a 20-story building. It contains **massive** stone doors that could only be opened or closed from the inside. This piece of evidence leads experts to believe that the underground city was built to protect the city's residents from enemies. More than 20,000 people could hide inside it. Over 600 doors lead to the city, hidden under and around existing homes.

C The hidden city had its own religious centers, livestock stables,[2] kitchens, and even schools. Wells, water tanks, and at least 15,000 air shafts[3] made the city a comfortable place. However, experts are not sure exactly how old the underground city is, because any records of its construction and use have disappeared.

[1]**renovations:** works that improve the design or condition of a house or building
[2]**stable:** a place to keep horses and cows
[3]**shaft:** an opening that goes all the way through a building

▲ **Rock formations called "fairy chimneys" can be found throughout the Cappadocia region in Turkey.**

D Until recently, Derinkuyu was the largest known underground city in Cappadocia. In 2013, however, construction workers **discovered** another underground city during the building of a housing project. This city—**located** beneath the city of Nevşehir—is one of the largest known underground cities in the world. According to researchers, this newly discovered **ancient** city could cover over 450,000 square meters and is over 110 meters deep. This means that using only simple tools, the ancient builders dug an area big enough for 65 soccer fields, and deep enough to contain a 35-story building!

E Researchers have found **artifacts** in this city such as tools and bowls. These artifacts suggest that the city is probably up to 5,000 years old. Like Derinkuyu, it was probably built as a place where people could stay safe during times of war.

F In the future, other people may **experience** the same excitement that the homeowner and the construction workers felt. There are already more than 30 known underground cities in the Cappadocia region, but experts believe there may be more than 200. So there are likely to be other hidden wonders, just waiting to be discovered.

▼ **Visitors exploring the underground city of Derinkuyu**

UNDERSTANDING THE READING

A Match each paragraph (A–F) to its main idea.

UNDERSTANDING
MAIN IDEAS

1. _____ There are likely to be many more underground cities in Turkey that have not yet been found.

2. _____ Scientists don't know how old the city is, but it seemed to have enough resources for its people.

3. _____ A man in Turkey discovered something surprising beneath his house.

4. _____ The artifacts found in the city below Nevşehir helped scientists work out its age and purpose.

5. _____ The structure of the hidden city suggests that people used the underground city to hide from danger.

6. _____ Workers found an underground city in Turkey that was bigger than Derinkuyu.

B Complete the chart about the two underground cities in Turkey. If the information is not in the reading, write "not given."

UNDERSTANDING
DETAILS

	Derinkuyu	below Nevşehir
Where is it located?		
Who discovered it?	a resident in the city	
How deep is it?		
How old is it?		
How many people could live there?		
What might be the purpose of the city?		

> **CRITICAL THINKING** When writers make an **analogy**, they compare something to another thing that is easier to understand. For example, to help a reader imagine the length of a blue whale, writers could say "A blue whale is about 24 meters long—around the length of two buses."

C Look back at paragraphs B and D in the reading passage. Find an analogy in each paragraph and underline it. What does each analogy help the reader understand?

CRITICAL THINKING:
UNDERSTANDING
ANALOGIES

Paragraph B: the **depth** / **area** of the city

Paragraph D: the **area** / **volume** and **depth** / **age** of the city

D Look back at paragraph E in the reading passage. What analogy could you use to describe the age of the city? Discuss your ideas with a partner.

CRITICAL THINKING:
APPLYING

That's as old as …   *That's older than …*

DEVELOPING READING SKILLS

> **READING SKILL** Identifying Facts and Speculations
>
> There are certain words and expressions you can look out for to distinguish between facts and speculations. A **fact** is an idea that has been proven to be true. A **speculation** is a guess. It might be based on evidence, but has not yet been proven. Writers use expressions such as *think, probably, possibly,* and *may* when talking about things they are not sure about.

CATEGORIZING **A** Read the paragraph about Ibn Battuta below. Then decide whether each piece of information is a fact (F) or speculation (S).

Ibn Battuta was one of the world's greatest explorers. He was born in 1304 in Tangier, Morocco. At the age of 21, he left home to travel across unexplored parts of Africa and Asia. His journey took him to places such as Cairo, Iraq, and Delhi. He may also have visited Beijing around 1346, although some historians think this is unlikely. After traveling almost 120,000 kilometers over a period of 29 years, he returned to Morocco and told people of his travels. We know little about Battuta's life after he stopped traveling—some say he may have worked as a judge. Battuta probably died in 1368 or 1369, and his final resting place is unknown.

Ibn Battuta (right) on a visit to Mongolia

1. where Battuta was from   F   S
2. how old Battuta was when he left home   F   S
3. whether Battuta visited Beijing   F   S
4. how many years Battuta traveled   F   S
5. how Battuta lived after returning home   F   S
6. when Battuta died   F   S

CATEGORIZING **B** Look back at the reading passage on pages 125–126. Decide whether each of the following pieces of information is a fact (F) or speculation (S).

1. the year Derinkuyu's underground city was discovered   F   S
2. who discovered the underground cities   F   S
3. the age of the underground cities   F   S
4. why the two underground cities were built   F   S
5. the number of underground cities in Cappadocia   F   S

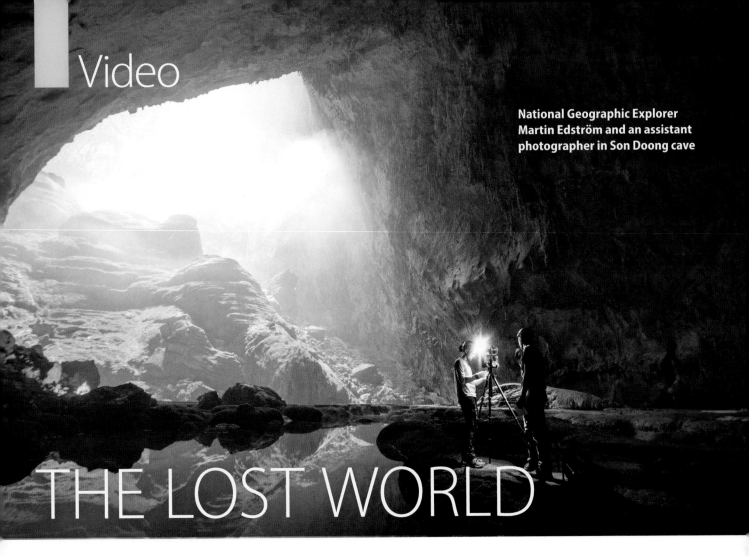

Video

National Geographic Explorer
**Martin Edström and an assistant
photographer in Son Doong cave**

THE LOST WORLD

BEFORE VIEWING

A Work with a partner. Read the title and look at the photo. How big do you think the cave is? Use an analogy to describe your ideas.

PREDICTING

B Read the information about Son Doong. Then answer the questions.

LEARNING ABOUT
THE TOPIC

At more than five kilometers long, Son Doong is one of the largest caves in the world. The cave—located in Vietnam—was created millions of years ago when river water caused the rock under the mountain to become soft and fall apart. A man called Ho Khanh discovered Son Doong in 1991, but he didn't know how to enter it. As a result, the cave remained a mystery. In 2009, a team of British cavers began to explore Son Doong with the help of Ho Khanh. A year later, a different team of cavers visited, and became the first people to explore the entire length of the cave.

1. Where is the cave? _____

2. Is the cave natural or man-made? _____

3. Who were the first people to enter the cave? _____

4. What do you think explorers might find in the cave? _____

_____

C The words in **bold** below are used in the video. Read the sentences. Then match each word to its definition.

> The Mariana Trench is a **vast** underwater valley.
>
> A country's traditional art and music are usually an important part of its **heritage**.
>
> As a result of globalization, small businesses may be under **threat** from international companies.

1. _____ (adj) very wide or big

2. _____ (n) a possibility of something bad happening

3. _____ (n) something from the past that still has cultural importance

WHILE VIEWING

A ▶ Watch the video. Why does Edström want to take pictures of the cave? Circle the most suitable answer.

    a. to encourage more tourists to visit the cave

    b. to help future explorers find their way through it

    c. to make people aware of the cave so they will want to protect it

B ▶ Watch the video again. Answer the questions (1–4).

  1. What is true about the pictures Edström and his team took?

    a. They show the cave from all angles.   b. They were taken using a flying robot.

  2. What is an example of a dangerous thing the team had to do?

    a. avoid snakes   b. cross a river in the dark

  3. Why is one of the sinkholes called "Watch out for dinosaurs"?

    a. Dinosaur bones were found there.   b. The area seemed like a different world.

  4. What have scientists discovered in the cave?

    a. new types of insects and fish   b. evidence of early humans

AFTER VIEWING

A Discuss these questions with a partner.

  1. Would you like to visit Son Doong? Why or why not?

  2. What are some advantages and disadvantages of allowing tourists to visit the cave?

B Work with a partner. What analogy was mentioned in the video caption? What did it describe?

The analogy described the **size / age / importance** of the cave by stating that

_____ could

_____ .

Reading 2

PREPARING TO READ

A The words in **blue** below are used in the reading passage on pages 132–133. Read the paragraph. Then match the correct form of each word to its definition.

BUILDING VOCABULARY

Scientists have always been interested in knowing if life **exists** outside of Earth. The **universe** is **extremely** large, so there is a chance that there could be other forms of life. In 2017, scientists found seven Earth-size planets located 40 light years away. This discovery may bring us closer to answering the question of life beyond Earth.

1. _____ (adv) very, really

2. _____ (v) to live or be present in a particular place

3. _____ (n) everything that is in space, such as stars and planets

B Complete the sentences using the words in the box. Use a dictionary to help you.

BUILDING VOCABULARY

run out	challenging	creatures	risk	surface

1. Underwater cave exploration can be _____ and dangerous, and divers often _____ their lives on expeditions.

2. Divers have to come back up to the _____ before they _____ of oxygen.

3. The bottom of the Mariana Trench is completely dark and very cold, but there are some _____ that are able to live there.

C Discuss these questions with a partner.

USING VOCABULARY

1. Do you think that life might **exist** on other planets in the **universe**? If so, what kind of life do you think could exist?

2. What are some places that are **extremely** difficult to live in? Why?

D Look at the photo and read the first paragraph of the reading on pages 132–133. What are some challenges blue hole explorers could face? Discuss with a partner. Then check your ideas as you read the passage.

PREDICTING

_____

_____

_____

INTO THE UNKNOWN

A In the early 19th century, much of the world was still unexplored. Today, most places on the surface of the Earth have been mapped. Some places, however, are still waiting to be discovered. Some of these are underground, in deep caves called blue holes.

B A blue hole is a special kind of underwater cave. It can be found inland[1] or in the sea. The hole forms when the earth above a cave falls in and water fills the space. Some of the world's most spectacular[2] blue holes are located in the Bahamas. The islands there may have more than a thousand blue holes. Blue holes can be very deep. For example, Dean's Blue Hole, one of the deepest blue holes in the world, is over 200 meters deep.

C An inland blue hole's water is very still and has different layers. A layer of fresh rainwater floats on top of salt water. The fresh water keeps oxygen from the atmosphere from reaching the salt water. Brightly colored bacteria live where the two layers meet.

D Diving into blue holes is extremely dangerous. Near the top of a blue hole, there is a layer of poisonous gas. This gas causes itching, dizziness, and—in large amounts—death. Divers must also be fast. They have to get in and out of a cave before their oxygen runs out. Additionally, it is very dark in these caves, so it is very easy to get lost. Divers therefore have to follow a guideline[3] as they swim through a blue hole. If they lose the guideline, they may not find their way back out of the cave.

E If blue holes are so dangerous, why do explorers and scientists risk their lives to explore them? One reason is that these

Photographer Wes C. Skiles took this
photo of a blue hole in the Bahamas.

underwater caves can provide valuable
scientific information. They provide clues
about geology, archaeology, and biology. For
example, some blue hole creatures, such as
the remipede, probably haven't changed for
millions of years.

F

The blue holes could even provide clues
about astrobiology—the study of life in the
universe. For example, divers have found
bacteria there that can live without oxygen.
Astrobiologist Kevin Hand says the bacteria in
blue holes may be similar to forms of life that
might exist on Jupiter's fourth largest moon,
Europa. Similar life forms probably existed on
Earth billions of years ago. "Our study of life's
extremes on Earth," he says, can help increase

"our understanding of habitable environments
off Earth."

In addition, the oxygen-free environment
of the blue holes preserves bones of humans
and animals that fell into the caves long ago.
By studying blue holes, we can understand
G   what life was like in prehistoric[4] times. As
cave diver Kenny Broad says, "I can think
of no other environment on Earth that is so
challenging to explore and gives us back so
much scientifically."

[1] inland: away from the ocean
[2] spectacular: very impressive or dramatic
[3] guideline: a line or a rope that someone follows to go from one
   place to another
[4] prehistoric: (people and things) existing at a time before
   information was written down

UNDERSTANDING THE READING

UNDERSTANDING PURPOSE

A Match each section of the passage to its purpose.

_____ 1. Paragraphs A–B
a. to explain the importance of studying blue holes

_____ 2. Paragraph C
b. to show why blue hole exploration is challenging

_____ 3. Paragraph D
c. to describe the structure of a blue hole

_____ 4. Paragraphs E–G
d. to explain what blue holes are and how they are formed

SUMMARIZING

B Circle the correct words to complete the summary about blue holes.

Blue holes are caves that are [1] **underwater / high up in the mountains**. They were formed millions of years ago when [2] **huge earthquakes happened / the land above them fell in** and water entered the space. Blue holes are located on land or in the sea. Many of them are very deep and the water inside the holes is usually very [3] **rough / calm**. Although exploring blue holes is dangerous, many scientists still risk their lives to dive into them. They think that blue holes can tell us a lot about [4] **ancient life forms / how the oceans were formed**.

UNDERSTANDING DETAILS

C Complete the labels with information about an inland blue hole.

1. At the top of the blue hole is a layer of _____ water, while below it is a layer of _____ water. The top layer blocks _____ from entering the blue hole.

2. The gas near the top of the blue hole is _____, and breathing in too much of it can sometimes lead to _____.

3. _____ live in between the top and bottom layers.

4. It is very _____ in this part of a blue hole, so divers need to use a _____ when swimming.

CRITICAL THINKING: ANALYZING

D Look back at the reading passage on pages 132–133. Decide whether each piece of information is a fact (F) or speculation (S). Then discuss your ideas with a partner.

1. how blue holes are formed   F   S
2. the depth of Dean's Blue Hole   F   S
3. what the remipede looked like in the past   F   S
4. the types of life that we can find on Europa   F   S
5. the amount of oxygen in blue holes   F   S

Writing

EXPLORING WRITTEN ENGLISH

A Complete the sentences with the correct form of the verb in parentheses. Then underline the expressions that show an interest in or a desire to do something.

NOTICING

1. I would love to _____ (discover) a lost city someday.

2. I would like to _____ (study) archaeology because I want to _____ (learn) about ancient history.

3. I would be interested in _____ (visit) Turkey someday because I want to _____ (see) the underground cities.

4. I want to _____ (take) a tour of Paris and see the Louvre Museum.

5. I would be interested in _____ (learn) Spanish because I want to _____ (visit) Central America.

LANGUAGE FOR WRITING Expressing Interests and Desires

You can use certain expressions to introduce what you want to do. These include:

> *I would like to …*   *I would love to …*
>
> *I want to …*   *I would be interested in …*

Use the base form of the verb after *I would like to / I would love to*, and *I want to*. Use a gerund (*-ing* verb) after *I would be interested in*.

> I **would like to explore** the blue holes of the Bahamas because they look very interesting.

> I **would love to go** to Central America because I'm interested in Mayan history.

> I **would be interested in going** there because I am learning Spanish and I want to improve my Spanish language skills.

▼ **The site of one of Turkey's underground cities**

B Complete the chart with things you want to do in the next five years. Give reasons for each one.

Things you want to do	Two reasons why
visit Greece	1. see the ancient temples 2. eat Mediterranean food
1.	1. 2.
2.	1. 2.
3.	1. 2.

Use your notes in the chart above to write a sentence about each of the things that you want to do. Use the phrases in the Language for Writing box to help you.

Example:

I would like to visit Greece because I want to see the ancient temples and eat Mediterranean food.

1. _____

    _____

    _____

2. _____

    _____

    _____

3. _____

    _____

    _____

You can give examples to give more information about your supporting ideas. In Unit 6, you learned how to identify examples (*for example, for instance*). Here are more phrases that introduce examples:

To give an example, …
A famous/great example is …
One of the best examples is …

Sometimes, people use the short form "e.g." in their writing to introduce an example. You can use this in informal writing—such as in an email to a friend—but it may not always be appropriate in academic writing.

Note: In Units 2 and 3, you learned how to order and connect supporting ideas in a paragraph using *also*, *in addition*, and *finally*. You can use these words and phrases in this unit to organize your supporting ideas.

C Read the paragraph below. Use the phrases in the box to link supporting ideas and introduce examples.

> a famous example　　first of all　　for instance　　in addition

I would like to explore Australia for many reasons. [1] _____, there are a lot of interesting animals in Australia. I would love to see some of the amazing animals that live on the south coast. [2] _____ is the fairy penguin, the world's smallest species of penguin. [3] _____, Australia is a good place to study aboriginal culture. The Art Gallery of New South Wales, [4] _____, has an excellent collection of aboriginal art.

D Choose one thing you would like to do from exercise B. Expand on your sentence in B to include examples. Use the expressions from the Writing Skill box to help you.

Example:

I would like to visit Greece because I want to see the ancient temples. For example, I would love to see the Temple of Apollo at Delphi. I also really want to eat Mediterranean food, such as moussaka.

_____

_____

_____

_____

_____

_____

WRITING TASK

GOAL You are going to write a paragraph about the following topic:

Where would you most like to explore? Why would you like to go there?

BRAINSTORMING **A** Make a list of places you would like to explore or learn more about. Discuss your list with a partner.

_____

_____

_____

PLANNING **B** Follow these steps to make notes for your paragraph. Don't worry about grammar or spelling. Don't write complete sentences.

Step 1 Look at your brainstorming notes. Circle one place you want to write about.

Step 2 Write a topic sentence stating the place you are interested in going to.

Step 3 Think of three reasons that you want to explore this place. Note them in the outline as your supporting ideas.

Step 4 Think of an example or an explanation for each reason. Note them as your details.

OUTLINE

Topic sentence: _____

_____

Supporting Idea 1: _____

_____

Detail: _____

Supporting Idea 2: _____

_____

Detail: _____

Supporting Idea 3: _____

_____

Detail: _____

FIRST DRAFT **C** Use the information in the outline to write a first draft of your paragraph.

REVISING PRACTICE

The drafts below are similar to the one you are going to write.

What did the writer do in Draft 2 to improve the paragraph? Match the changes (a–d) to the highlighted parts.

a. expanded on an example
b. fixed an error with expressing an interest or a desire
c. added a linking expression to order ideas
d. added an expression for introducing an example

Draft 1

I would like to explore Australia for many reasons. First of all, there are many beautiful and unusual birds there. There are bright red and blue rosellas, a type of Australian parrot. It is a great place to go diving. A famous example is the Great Barrier Reef, which is filled with beautiful fish. Finally, I'm interested in learn more about the aboriginal culture of Australia. For instance, I would like to visit the Australia Museum in Sydney.

Draft 2

I would like to explore Australia for many reasons. First of all, there are many beautiful and unusual birds there. To give an example, there are bright red and blue rosellas, a type of Australian parrot. Second, it is a great place to go diving. A famous example is the Great Barrier Reef, which is filled with beautiful fish. Finally, I'm interested in learning more about the aboriginal culture of Australia. For instance, I would like to visit the Australia Museum in Sydney because it is one of the best places to see aboriginal art and artifacts.

D Now use the questions below to revise your paragraph.

REVISED DRAFT

- ☐ Did you use the correct expression for stating where you want to go?
- ☐ Did you use linking expressions for your supporting ideas?
- ☐ Did you include a detail for each supporting idea?
- ☐ Did you use the correct expressions for introducing examples?

◀ a rosella

EDITING PRACTICE

Read the information below.

In sentences expressing interest or desire, remember to:

• use the base form of the verb after *would like to, would love to,* and *want to.*

• use a gerund after *be interested in.*

Correct one mistake with language for expressing interest in each of the sentences (1–5).

1. I would like visit the Amazon rain forest because there are many different types of animals there.

2. I would love to exploring New York City because it is full of interesting art and culture.

3. My brother and I are interested in to visit Russia because we want to learn more about Russian history.

4. My sister would like traveling to every continent because she loves to learn about different cultures.

5. My parents would like to go to Turkey one day because they want to exploring the underground cities.

FINAL DRAFT **E** Follow these steps to write a final draft.

1. Check your revised draft for mistakes with language for expressing interest.

2. Now use the checklist on page 218 to write a final draft. Make any other necessary changes.

UNIT REVIEW

Answer the following questions.

1. Which place mentioned in this unit would you be most interested in exploring? Why?

_____

_____

_____

2. What are some words that show that something is a speculation?

_____

_____

_____

3. Do you remember the meanings of these words? Check (✓) the ones you know. Look back at the unit and review the ones you don't know.

Reading 1:

☐ ancient   ☐ artifact   ☐ deep

☐ discover   ☐ experience   ☐ hidden

☐ located [AWL] ☐ massive   ☐ region [AWL]

☐ underground

Reading 2:

☐ challenging [AWL] ☐ creature   ☐ exist

☐ extremely   ☐ risk   ☐ run out

☐ surface   ☐ universe

MUSIC WITH A MESSAGE

8

Musician Ta'Kaiya Blaney encourages people to care for the environment.

THINK AND DISCUSS

1 Who are some of your favorite musicians? What do you like about them?
2 In what ways do you think musicians can change the world?

A **Read the information on these pages and answer the questions.**

1. Have you seen or listened to any benefit concerts? What do you remember about them?

2. Why do you think musicians take part in benefit events?

B **Match the correct form of the words in blue to their definitions.**

_____ (n) a group of people watching a concert or other event

_____ (v) to suggest that someone act in a certain way

_____ (v) to do something in front of people to entertain them

BRINGING THE WORLD TOGETHER

For more than 40 years, musicians have helped bring people around the world together. For example, benefit concerts raise money and make people aware of global problems such as poverty or environmental issues.

Live 8

Live 8 was a group of benefit concerts that were held on the same day in 2005. More than a thousand musicians **performed** in 9 countries, including France, Japan, and South Africa. The goal was to raise money for poor countries.

Oxjam

Oxjam raises money for Oxfam, an organization that fights poverty around the world. Every October, Oxjam holds music events around the United Kingdom and Ireland. It also **encourages** people to hold events in their own communities.

Live Earth

The purpose of Live Earth was to help make people aware of climate change. In 2007, 150 performers appeared in concerts on every continent, including Antarctica. **Audiences** in over 130 countries watched the concerts on TV.

Red Rocks Amphitheatre in Colorado, U.S.A., has been the venue for some of the biggest names in world music.

Reading 1

PREPARING TO READ

BUILDING
VOCABULARY

A The words in **blue** below are used in the reading passage on pages 145–146. Read the paragraph. Then match the sentence parts to make definitions.

Many musicians never give up on their love for music even during difficult times. The **composer** Ludwig van Beethoven, for example, was deaf. Even though he started to lose his hearing in his 20s, Beethoven continued creating many pieces of classical music for a variety of **instruments**, such as piano and violin. Rick Allen, the drummer from Def Leppard, lost his left arm in a car accident. Although he was **disabled**, he continued to perform with a special drum set which allowed him to use his left leg to play the drums.

1. If you are a **composer**, _____   a. you can play music with.

2. An **instrument** is something _____   b. you write music.

3. If you are physically **disabled**, _____   c. you are unable to do an activity such as walking or seeing.

BUILDING
VOCABULARY

B Complete the sentences using the words in the box. Use a dictionary to help you.

> energetic   documentary   positive   appearance

1. A(n) _____ person is very active and does not feel tired easily.

2. We can describe a person's _____ with words like *short* or *pretty*.

3. Someone who is _____ believes that good things will happen.

4. A(n) _____ is a movie that gives facts and information about a topic.

USING
VOCABULARY

C Discuss these questions with a partner.

1. Which famous **composers** do you know? What do you think of their music?

2. Where in your town can you go to listen to musicians **performing** live music?

BRAINSTORMING

D Why is music important? How can music help people? Note your ideas. Then discuss with a partner.

_____

_____

PREDICTING

E Read the first paragraph of the reading passage on page 145. What do you think are some challenges disabled musicians face? Discuss with a partner. Then check your ideas as you read the passage.

_____

Staff Benda Bilili
performing in London

THE POWER OF MUSIC

🎧 15

A   In 2004, two French filmmakers were working in Kinshasa, the capital of the Democratic Republic of the Congo (DRC). One day, they found a group of musicians performing on the streets. But these were not ordinary street musicians. Most of the band members were disabled, and they played music with homemade instruments.

THE MESSAGE IN THE MUSIC

B   The band is called Staff Benda Bilili. The founders[1] of the band are Coco—the band's composer—and Ricky. Junana, the group's choreographer, designs the group's stage performances. Coude is a bass player and singer. A non-disabled member, Roger, plays the satongé—a one-string guitar. He made the instrument out of a tin can, a fish basket, and an electrical wire.

C   The band's name, Staff Benda Bilili, means "look beyond appearances" in the local language. It also describes the group's mission. Staff Benda Bilili's audience was at first made up of poor street people. The band wanted to tell its audience to be positive and strong, even in difficult situations.

D   "Our songs encourage kids to go to school, encourage people to work hard," says Ricky. "The message of our music is that if you want to do something with your life, you need to take things in your own hands."

[1]founder: a creator of something

The band members themselves are examples of their message. They don't see themselves as disabled. Instead, they see themselves as rock musicians. Their energetic performances show this. For example, when the group is playing, Junana sometimes jumps out of his wheelchair and dances around the stage on his hands.

FROM THE STREETS TO THE WORLD

The filmmakers Florent de la Tullaye and Renaud Barret were amazed by Staff Benda Bilili's music and their life stories. So they decided to make a documentary about the band. The film follows the band as it plays its music in Kinshasa, a city that had been through many wars.[2] These wars affected millions of people in Kinshasa and elsewhere in the DRC. The documentary illustrates how Staff Benda Bilili's music helped people survive in this very difficult environment.

The film also shows the power of Staff Benda Bilili's music. The band members often wrote songs about the life problems they faced. Many of the songs offer solutions to the problems. For example, "Polio" is about living with polio[3] and getting around the city on crutches. It also tells parents the importance of vaccination for their children.

The documentary follows Staff Benda Bilili as it goes from playing in the streets of Kinshasa to playing in large European cities. Because of the film, the band became well known, and it was able to give hope to people around the world through its music.

[2] The **Second Congo War** (1998–2003) caused the deaths of as many as 5.4 million people, more than any other war since World War II.
[3] **polio:** a disease that sometimes makes people unable to use their legs

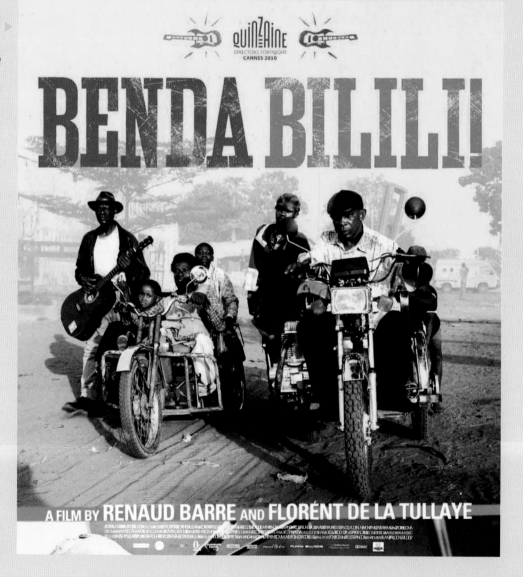

The film *Benda Bilili* shows how the band overcame life's difficulties to become successful musicians.

UNDERSTANDING THE READING

A What is the main idea of each section of the passage? Circle the correct answers.

UNDERSTANDING MAIN IDEAS

1. **The Message in the Music**

   a. Staff Benda Bilili's music encourages people who live in difficult circumstances.

   b. Staff Benda Bilili encourages people to play music to deal with their problems.

2. **From the Streets to the World**

   a. Staff Benda Bilili made a film about their lives as musicians in Kinshasa.

   b. A film about Staff Benda Bilili brought the band's message to people around the world.

B Read the sentences about Staff Benda Bilili below. Circle T for *true* or F for *false*.

UNDERSTANDING DETAILS

1.	The band members made their own instruments.	T	F
2.	All members of Staff Benda Bilili are disabled.	T	F
3.	A satongé is a musical instrument similar to a drum.	T	F
4.	At first, Staff Benda Bilili performed music for poor people.	T	F
5.	The band's stage performances show how they overcome their disabilities.	T	F

C Find and underline the following words in the reading. Use context to identify their meanings. Then match each word to its definition (1–3).

CRITICAL THINKING: INFERRING MEANING

choreographer (paragraph B) **mission** (paragraph C) **vaccination** (paragraph G)

1. _____ (n) a goal

2. _____ (n) someone who creates dances

3. _____ (n) an injection to protect against a disease

> **CRITICAL THINKING** Writers often use **idiomatic language**—phrases that have a different meaning from the meaning of the actual words used. Look at the information around an idiomatic phrase to help you understand what it means.

D Read the sentences containing idiomatic expressions. Choose the most suitable meaning for each **bold** phrase.

CRITICAL THINKING: INTERPRETING IDIOMATIC LANGUAGE

1. The band's name, Staff Benda Bilili, means "**look beyond appearances**."

   a. Judge people based on what they do and not how they look.

   b. The way people look tells you a lot about them.

2. Ricky says, "The message of our music is that . . . you need to **take things in your own hands**."

   a. It's better to fix broken things than to buy new ones.

   b. Take action on your own and don't rely on other people.

DEVELOPING READING SKILLS

READING SKILL Taking Notes

Taking notes helps you understand the main ideas of a reading passage and how supporting details relate to those ideas. It also helps you gather information for writing assignments and tests. One way to take notes is to identify main ideas and supporting details using a graphic organizer, such as a simple chart.

Abbreviations and symbols make note-taking easier and faster. You can abbreviate (shorten) words any way you want (as long as you understand your abbreviations). Some common abbreviations and symbols include:

& or + :	and	w/ :	with	e.g. or ex. :	example
→ :	leads to/causes	= :	is/means	b/c :	because

TAKING NOTES **A** Complete the chart with notes from the passage on pages 145–146.

Paragraph	Main Idea / Topic	Supporting Details
B	the members of Staff Benda Bilili (SBB)	Ricky (co-founder), Junana (choreographer), Coco (co-founder & _____), Coude (bass player & singer), Roger (plays satongé)
C–D	the group's _____	- SBB = "look beyond _____" - at first, audience incl. very poor people - goal: to tell their audience to stay _____ in difficult times
E	_____ are examples of their message	- see themselves as _____ rather than disabled people - performances are very energetic
F	a _____ was made about the band	- shows SBB playing music in Kinshasa, a city that has seen many _____ - shows how SBB's music helped people survive the difficult environment
G	the power of SBB's music	- SBB writes songs about the _____ they have in their lives, e.g., one song was about living with _____
H	the impact of the film	- SBB became famous in Europe - their music gives _____ to people around the world

APPLYING **B** Choose a reading passage from an earlier unit. Create a chart like the one above to note the passage's main ideas and supporting details.

American artists George Clinton and Parliament Funkadelic play at a WOMAD festival in the United Kingdom.

Video

WORLD MUSIC

BEFORE VIEWING

A Look at the title and the caption. What do you think WOMAD stands for? Discuss with a partner.

PREDICTING

B Read the information about WOMAD. Then discuss the questions with a partner.

LEARNING ABOUT THE TOPIC

Each year, artists from around the world perform at WOMAD, an international arts festival where people can enjoy music, arts, and dance from different countries. WOMAD festivals take place in many cities around the world. The first was held in England, but since then, more than 30 countries have held their own WOMAD event.

1. What do you think WOMAD aims to do?

   _____

2. Have you been to a similar concert? What was it like?

   _____

3. How do you think WOMAD concerts might be different from other kinds of concerts, like classical or rock concerts?

   _____

   _____

C The words in **bold** below are used in the video. Read the paragraph. Then match each word to its definition.

At WOMAD festivals, some bands play modern music like rock or rap, but others play more **traditional** music. People can also see paintings and artwork from international artists, and watch **stunning** performances by dancers. WOMAD encourages people to be **open-minded** about experiencing art and music from different countries and cultures.

1. _____ (adj) very impressive or beautiful

2. _____ (adj) existing for a long time without any change

3. _____ (adj) curious; interested to try new things

WHILE VIEWING

A ▶ Read the questions and watch the video. Then circle PG for *Peter Gabriel* or MC for *Marcello Colasurdo*.

1. Who co-founded WOMAD?   **PG**   **MC**

2. Who is preparing to perform at WOMAD?   **PG**   **MC**

3. Who compares his music to rap music?   **PG**   **MC**

B ▶ Watch the video again. Complete the notes about Spaccanapoli by circling the correct words.

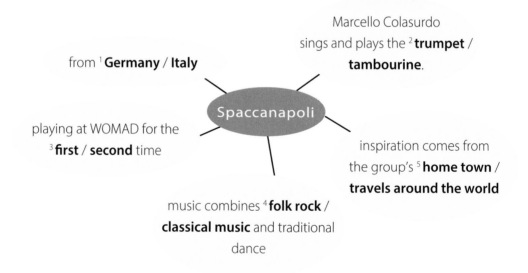

from [1] **Germany / Italy**

Marcello Colasurdo sings and plays the [2] **trumpet / tambourine**.

Spaccanapoli

playing at WOMAD for the [3] **first / second** time

inspiration comes from the group's [5] **home town / travels around the world**

music combines [4] **folk rock / classical music** and traditional dance

AFTER VIEWING

A Discuss this question with a partner: If you were organizing a WOMAD event in your country, which singers or bands from your country or culture would you invite?

B Work with a partner. How is WOMAD similar to and different from one of the events described on page 143?

Reading 2

PREPARING TO READ

A The words in **blue** below are used in the reading passage on pages 152–153. Complete the sentences with the correct form of the words.

BUILDING VOCABULARY

> If you **escape** from something, you get away from it.
>
> If you **improve** something, you make it better.
>
> An **issue** is an important topic that people have different views on.
>
> A **bond** between people is a strong connection or feeling of friendship.
>
> If you **rescue** someone, you save them from something bad.
>
> A **responsibility** is a job or task you have to do.
>
> A **situation** is what is happening at a particular time.
>
> If doctors or nurses **treat** someone with an illness, they try to make them well again.

1. One global _____ that affects our planet is climate change.

2. Medical technology such as X-ray machines can help doctors identify patients' problems and _____ them effectively.

3. A firefighter's _____ is to put out fires and _____ people from burning buildings.

4. People who work together in a difficult _____ often form a strong _____ .

5. Education and training can _____ the lives of people in poor countries. It can help them get jobs or start businesses, which may help them _____ a life of poverty.

B Discuss these questions with a partner: What do you think is one important social issue today? What are people doing to **improve** the situation?

USING VOCABULARY

_____

_____

_____

C Look at the photos and headings on pages 152–153. What kind of "change" do you think the musicians are hoping to inspire? Discuss with a partner. Then check your ideas as you read the passage.

PREDICTING

Sinikithemba means "we bring hope" in Zulu.

MUSIC FOR CHANGE

🎧 16

A From ending child slavery[1] to teaching people about AIDS and world peace, musicians around the world are spreading a message of hope.

Jason Mraz: Singing for Freedom

B "If my music can contribute to happiness, then that's my main **responsibility**," says American singer and songwriter Jason Mraz. But Mraz does more than make people happy. He wants to use his music to make a positive change and **improve** people's lives.

C In 2010, Mraz visited Ghana with an organization called Free the Slaves. Its goal is to stop child slavery, a serious **issue** in many parts of the world. In Ghana, parents who are very poor sometimes sell their own children into slavery.

D What inspired Mraz to visit Ghana? "It started with 'Freedom Song,' written by musician Luc Reynaud," he says. "I loved it, performed it, and passed it on to my friends at Free the Slaves." After seeing videos of kids in Ghana enjoying the song, he decided to visit. On his trip, he worked with James Kofi Annan—a former child slave. Mraz explains that Annan works to "**rescue** children, and get them back to health. [He also] works with their parents to make sure they can make a living so the children aren't **vulnerable**[2] to traffickers."[3]

Arn Chorn-Pond: Healing with Music

E As a child, Arn Chorn-Pond worked in a prison camp in Cambodia during the Khmer Rouge period.[4] Life in the camp was terrifying.

---

[1] A **slave** is someone who is owned by other people and works for them without being paid.

[2] Someone who is **vulnerable** is weak and without protection.

[3] A **trafficker** is someone who illegally buys or sells something.

Zinhle Thabethe: Bringing Hope

National Geographic Explorer Zinhle Thabethe is a lead singer of a South African group called the Sinikithemba Choir. The members of this choir have a strong **bond**: They are all HIV positive. Thabethe first

G learned she had HIV in 2002. A doctor told her he could not **treat** her condition because medicine was not widely available. But Thabethe did not give up, and she finally found a clinic that was able to help HIV/AIDS patients.

Thabethe and other members of the Sinikithemba Choir send a message of hope to people with HIV/AIDS. She feels that she understands their **situation**. "I know what they

H are going through, and can help support and guide them," she says. "Only by being open and asking for help will we know that we are not alone. If you have someone who will walk the journey with you, it is always easier."

Camp workers of all ages were badly treated by the guards. Many workers died as a result. Chorn-Pond stayed alive mainly because of his skills as a musician. The camp guards liked listening to him as he played his flute.

Chorn-Pond finally **escaped** into the jungle, where he lived alone for many months. Later, an American aid worker met him and took him to the United States. When Chorn-Pond grew up, he went back to Cambodia. He learned that

F many traditional musicians and dancers had died during the Khmer Rouge period. So Chorn-Pond is working with older musicians to teach young Cambodians to play traditional music. In this way, he is helping a new generation keep their musical traditions alive.

[4] During the **Khmer Rouge period** (1975–1979), a political organization called Khmer Rouge governed Cambodia.

"[It is a] basic human right, to express yourself," says Chorn-Pond.

UNDERSTANDING THE READING

A Match the main ideas (1–4) to the paragraphs listed in the chart.

1. traveled overseas as part of his efforts to stop child slavery
2. is helping to keep traditional music alive
3. did not give up despite having a serious illness
4. used his musical skills to survive a dangerous period

Paragraph(s)	Main Idea	Supporting Details
C–D	Jason Mraz _____	went to _____ after seeing children enjoying "Freedom Song" worked with Annan, a former _____
E	Arn Chorn-Pond _____	played flute for _____ playing music helped C-P avoid being killed
F	Arn Chorn-Pond _____	returned to _____ as an adult works w/ _____ and teaches trad. music to _____
G	Zinhle Thabethe _____	a doctor told her that he _____ _____ she found a _____ that could help her

TAKING NOTES **B** Now complete the supporting details in the chart above using information from the reading passage.

CRITICAL THINKING:
INTERPRETING
IDIOMATIC
LANGUAGE

C Work with a partner. Zinhle Thabethe says, "If you have someone who will walk the journey with you, it is always easier." What do you think "walk the journey" means?

_____

_____

CRITICAL THINKING:
EVALUATING

D Look back at the reading passage. Which musician's social work do you think is most important? Why? Note your answer. Then discuss with a partner.

I think the issue of _____ is the most important because

_____

_____.

Writing

EXPLORING WRITTEN ENGLISH

A Read the sentences. Underline the words that introduce information about when an event happened.

NOTICING

1. The Live Earth event took place in 2007.
2. Thabethe first learned she had HIV in 2002.
3. Jason Mraz worked with James Kofi Annan during his visit to Ghana.
4. When Arn Chorn-Pond grew up, he went back to Cambodia.

LANGUAGE FOR WRITING Using Time Expressions

Here are a few words you can use to show when events happened in a person's life:

in + [year/phrase]   *during* + [phrase]   *when/while/after/before* + [clause]

*Yo-Yo Ma was born in Paris **in** 1955.*
*He started playing the cello **when** he was four years old.*
***After** he moved to New York, he attended the Juilliard School of Music.*
***During** his childhood, Ma performed music on TV and even played for American presidents.*

When a time phrase or clause comes first in a sentence, a comma separates it from the rest of the sentence.

***In 1998**, he started an organization.* → *He started an organization **in 1998**.*
***When he was four years old**, he learned to play the cello.* → *He learned to play the cello **when he was four years old**.*

B Complete the sentences with a time expression from the Language for Writing box. Use the information in this unit to choose the correct words. There may be more than one possible answer.

1. The first WOMAD festival was held _____ 1982.
2. Staff Benda Bilili formed _____ they were living on the streets of Kinshasa.
3. Two French filmmakers discovered Staff Benda Bilili _____ they were working in Kinshasa.
4. Staff Benda Bilili become famous around Europe _____ people saw the film about them.
5. Jason Mraz visited Ghana _____ seeing how the children loved his performance of "Freedom Song."
6. Arn Chorn-Pond worked in a prison camp in Cambodia _____ the Khmer Rouge period.
7. Chorn-Pond played music for the guards _____ he was in a prison camp.

C Make a list of three important events in your life. Then write a sentence about each one using time expressions in the Language for Writing box on page 155.

_____

_____

_____

_____

_____

_____

_____

_____

> ### WRITING SKILL Planning a Narrative Paragraph
>
> When you write a narrative paragraph, you describe important events in the order that they happened. To plan a narrative paragraph about a person, for example, follow these steps:
>
> **Step 1** Make a timeline of events in the person's life. Include major life events such as when they were born. Also include important achievements—things that make the person interesting or admirable.
>
> **Step 2** Check your timeline. Delete unrelated or uninteresting events, but make sure you have enough events to give a clear picture of the person's life.
>
> **Step 3** Think of a topic sentence. In this case, it should be a general statement about the person that expresses what makes them special.

D Cross out three sentences that do not belong in this paragraph about Ta'Kaiya Blaney (the singer pictured on page 141).

Ta'Kaiya Blaney is a musician who is working to protect the environment and make people aware of climate change. Climate change refers to a long-term change in global weather patterns. Blaney was born in 2001 in Tla A'min Nation, an indigenous community in Canada. The community has over 1,000 people. When she was 8, she started training with a voice coach. By the time she was 10, she released her first song, _Shallow Waters_. Despite her young age, Blaney has spoken at many environmental conferences around the world. In 2011, she spoke at the TUNZA United Nations Children and Youth Conference on the Environment. Over the next three years, she was a speaker at a number of United Nations conferences in Rio de Janeiro and New York. The United Nations headquarters is in New York. Blaney was also featured in several films that raise awareness of environmental issues, such as _Saving My Tomorrow_ and _Konnected.tv_. She continues to create music that spreads positive messages. In 2015, she performed her song, _Earth Revolution_, in Paris.

E Read the paragraph about the life of the composer A.R. Rahman. Circle the event that is in the wrong order, and draw an arrow to where it should belong. Cross out one event that is not relevant.

(1) A.R. Rahman was born in Madras, India, in 1967. (2) When he was 11 years old, he dropped out of school and became a professional musician. (3) Even though he was young, he played music with some very famous Indian musicians, including Zakir Hussain. (4) After he came back to India, he started composing music for TV programs, advertisements, and later, movies. (5) Rahman received a scholarship to study music at Oxford University. (6) Oxford University is a famous university in England. (7) After Rahman got his degree, he returned to India. (8) In 2009, Rahman won an Academy Award for his music for the movie *Slumdog Millionaire.*

F Choose the most suitable topic sentence for the paragraph in exercise E.

   a. A.R. Rahman is one of the world's best-known Indian musicians.

   b. A.R. Rahman is known for his contributions to charity.

   c. A.R. Rahman produced many famous pieces of music throughout his career.

A.R. Rahman mixes traditional music with modern electronic sounds.

WRITING TASK

> **GOAL** You are going to write a paragraph on the following topic:
> Describe the life of a musician or a performer you admire.

BRAINSTORMING **A** Think of a musician or performer that you admire. List as many events or achievements in their life as you can. Then share your ideas with a partner.

Musician / Performer	
Main life events / Key achievements	

PLANNING **B** Follow these steps to make notes for your paragraph. Don't worry about grammar or spelling. Don't write complete sentences.

Step 1 Use your notes in exercise A to make a timeline of events in this person's life. Include at least four events.

Step 2 Make sure the events are in a logical order. Do all the events help explain what you admire about the person? Delete any that are not relevant.

Step 3 Write the timeline events in the outline. Include some details about each one.

Step 4 Write a topic sentence that states what you admire about the person.

OUTLINE

Topic sentence: _____

_____

Event 1 / Details: _____

_____

Event 2 / Details: _____

_____

Event 3 / Details: _____

_____

Event 4 / Details: _____

_____

FIRST DRAFT **C** Use the information in your outline to write a first draft of your paragraph.

REVISING PRACTICE

The drafts below are similar to the one you are going to write.

What did the writer do in Draft 2 to improve the paragraph? Match the changes (a–d) to the highlighted parts.

a. improved the topic sentence
b. corrected the order of events
c. corrected a time expression
d. deleted unnecessary information

Draft 1

I admire the Chinese-American cellist Yo-Yo Ma. Ma was born in Paris, France, in 1955. He started playing the cello when he was only four years old. During he was seven, he moved with his family to New York City. He performed professionally while he was studying, and he started to become a famous cellist during that time. In New York, Ma attended the Juilliard School of Music. After that, he studied at Harvard University. In 1998, Ma founded an organization called the Silk Road Project because he wanted to use music to bring people from all over the world together. The Silk Road was an ancient road that connected Asia, the Middle East, and Europe. With the organization, Ma gives cross-cultural music performances with musicians from places like Iran, Mongolia, and Italy. Through his work, Ma is helping people all over the world appreciate different types of music.

Draft 2

I admire the Chinese-American cellist Yo-Yo Ma because he connects people around the world through music. Ma was born in Paris, France, in 1955. He started playing the cello when he was only four years old. When he was seven, he moved with his family to New York City. In New York, Ma attended the Juilliard School of Music. After that, he studied at Harvard University. He performed professionally while he was studying, and he started to become a famous cellist during that time. In 1998, Ma founded an organization called the Silk Road Project because he wanted to use music to bring people from all over the world together. With the organization, Ma gives cross-cultural music performances with musicians from places like Iran, Mongolia, and Italy. Through his work, Ma is helping people all over the world appreciate different types of music.

D Now use the questions below to revise your paragraph. REVISED DRAFT

☐ Did you include a topic sentence about the person you are writing about?

☐ Did you put the events in order of when they happened?

☐ Do all the events relate to the person's life?

☐ Did you use time expressions correctly?

EDITING PRACTICE

Read the information below.

In sentences with time expressions, remember:
- to use *when*, *while*, *after*, and *before* at the start of a clause.
- that *during* is followed by a noun phrase, e.g., *the concert*, and not a clause.
- to use a comma when a time phrase or clause comes first in a sentence.

Correct one mistake with time expressions in each of the sentences (1–6).

1. The violinist Itzhak Perlman became famous after he performed on TV during 1958.

2. In 1998 Beyoncé's father quit his job to manage Destiny's Child.

3. Miles Davis moved to New York City to attend Juilliard, in 1945.

4. After Jay Z, heard Rihanna sing, he gave her a recording contract.

5. Lady GaGa was interested in acting before, she decided to become a singer.

6. Adele composed her first song during she was 16 years old.

FINAL DRAFT **E** **Follow these steps to write a final draft.**

1. Check your revised draft for mistakes with time expressions.

2. Now use the checklist on page 218 to write a final draft. Make any other necessary changes.

UNIT REVIEW

Answer the following questions.

1. Which musician/performer in this unit do you think is making the most positive impact? Why?

_____

_____

_____

2. What does a narrative describe?

_____

_____

_____

3. Do you remember the meanings of these words? Check (✓) the ones you know. Look back at the unit and review the ones you don't know.

Reading 1:

☐ appearance ☐ audience ☐ composer
☐ disabled ☐ documentary ☐ encourage
☐ energetic AWL ☐ instrument ☐ perform
☐ positive AWL

Reading 2:

☐ bond AWL ☐ escape ☐ improve
☐ issue AWL ☐ rescue ☐ responsibility
☐ situation ☐ treat

ANIMAL BEHAVIOR

A mandrill, the largest
species of monkey

THINK AND DISCUSS

1   What types of animals do you often see?
What are they usually doing?
2   What can humans do that animals cannot
do? What can some animals do that
humans cannot do?

A Read the information on these pages and answer the questions.

1. What are some skills that chimpanzees have?

2. How do dogs help people?

3. What other animals are close to humans? In what ways?

B Match the correct form of the words in blue to their definitions.

_____ (n) a person who has the right to have something

_____ (n) an animal that people keep at home

_____ (n) someone who spends time with you,
such as a friend

CLOSE TO US

Scientist Dr. Jane Goodall interacts with a chimpanzee named Jou Jou.

In terms of biology, non-human primates—such as great apes and monkeys—are the closest animals to human beings. Our closest relative is the chimpanzee. According to scientists, humans and chimpanzees share 96 percent of their DNA. Chimpanzees and humans also share several behavioral characteristics, such as living in social groups and using tools.

However, non-human primates are wild animals, and rarely live with or near people. Dogs, on the other hand, have lived and worked closely with humans for over 10,000 years. Dogs are more than just **companions** and house **pets**. Many dogs also have jobs such as guarding homes, performing police and rescue work, and helping **owners** with disabilities. Dogs cannot think like humans or use tools like some primates, but they are an important part of many people's everyday lives. In some ways, perhaps, they are "closer" to us than our nearest relatives.

Reading 1

PREPARING TO READ

BUILDING
VOCABULARY

A The words in **blue** below are used in the reading passage on pages 165–166. Read the paragraph. Then match the correct form of each word or phrase to its definition.

Many pet owners today send their dogs to schools where dog **trainers** teach them basic commands. Dog training is a relatively new **profession**, but did you know that the idea has been around for more than 2,000 years? In around 116–27 B.C., a Roman farmer called Marcus Varro wrote about the best **approaches** to training farm dogs. From his writings, it is clear that dogs received different training for different farm jobs. It also seems that trainers of this time had already **worked out** that it was best to start training dogs from a very young age.

1. _____ (n) a type of job that requires special skills

2. _____ (n) a person who teaches certain skills

3. _____ (n) a way to deal with something

4. _____ (v) to solve or understand something after overcoming problems

BUILDING
VOCABULARY

B Complete the sentences using the words from the box. Use a dictionary to help you.

> confused   angry   powerful

1. The CEO is one of the most _____ people in a company.

2. When training a puppy, you need to have patience and avoid getting _____ when it does something wrong.

3. The instructions on the product packaging were unclear, so I'm _____ about how it should be used.

USING
VOCABULARY

C Note your answer to this question: What skills do you think a professional dog **trainer** needs to have? Then discuss with a partner.

_____

_____

SKIMMING

D Skim the questions in the interview with Cesar Millan on pages 165–166. Check (✓) the topic(s) that the interview covers. Then check your answers as you read the passage.

☐ 1. some reasons that people choose to have particular types of dogs

☐ 2. how and why Millan became a dog trainer

☐ 3. some things that dogs can teach us

☐ 4. some differences between human and dog behavior

"I train people. I rehabilitate dogs."

THE ANIMAL TRAINER

🎧 17

Mexican-born animal **trainer** Cesar Millan is one of the world's best-known animal trainers. On his TV shows, Millan helps dogs and dog **owners** deal with their problems. He helps **angry** and scared dogs become good **companions**. He also helps **confused** humans become confident, happy dog owners.

What is the biggest mistake we make with dogs?

We humanize dogs. We hold conversations with them as if they were people ...
A dog doesn't know it lives in Beverly Hills or how much we spend on it.

Why do people like certain kinds of dogs?

It's about what they want from another human but can't get, so they get it from a dog.

So a person gets a pit bull as a pet because ...?

Because it represents power, strength, masculinity[1]—like driving a Ferrari.

And a small poodle?

Because it's feminine. Decorative.[2]

So people get dogs that are like them?

I walk into a home, and I don't have to hear much. I see the dog, and I know who you are. It's a mirror.

[1] **Masculinity** means the characteristics thought to be typical of being a man. The opposite of masculinity is **femininity**.
[2] Something that is **decorative** looks pretty or attractive.

What is your approach to helping owners with their dog problems?

If you don't tell a dog what to do, it will tell you what to do. My clients[3] are **powerful**, they have Harvard degrees, they run [big corporations], but they can't control a dog. You don't ask a dog if it would like to go for a walk. You put on the leash[4] and go.

Is there any creature you can't rehabilitate?[5]

My father …. I want him to tell my mother, "I appreciate you. Thank you. I love you." But he can't, not in the machismo[6] culture of Mexico.

Can't you take your father for a walk and work out the issues?

No. He'd just run away.

How did your parents feel about your choice of profession?

They wanted me to become a professional, [like a] doctor [or] lawyer.

How does your father feel now that you've made it?

He still can't understand why Americans pay me for walking their dogs.

What are the lessons we learn from dogs?

To live in the moment. Also honesty . . . [and] integrity. They will never stab you in the back or lie to you.

Do dogs think and feel?

They feel—they are instinctual.[7] They don't think.

So which animal behaves better—humans or dogs?

Oh, dogs.

---

[3] A **client** receives a professional service in return for payment.
[4] A **leash** is a long, thin piece of material used to keep a dog under control.
[5] To **rehabilitate** someone means to help that person live a normal life again, e.g., following an illness.
[6] **Machismo** refers to a man's behavior when he is very proud of his masculinity.
[7] **Instinctual** actions are made according to feelings, rather than opinions or ideas.

Some working dogs are trained to rescue drowning people.

UNDERSTANDING THE READING

A Check (✓) the statements that you think Cesar Millan would agree with.

UNDERSTANDING MAIN IDEAS

☐ 1. Dog owners should treat their dogs like people.

☐ 2. A dog trainer has to work with both dogs and their owners.

☐ 3. Humans are easier to teach than dogs.

☐ 4. You can tell a lot about a person by meeting their dog.

B Circle the best options to complete the sentences.

UNDERSTANDING DETAILS

1. Millan says that many dog owners make the mistake of **treating dogs like people** / **allowing dogs in their bedrooms**.

2. People sometimes like certain dogs based on what they **like about** / **want from** other people.

3. According to Millan, people choose dogs that are **different from** / **similar to** them.

4. Millan thinks that some of his clients have problems with their dogs because they aren't **firm** / **patient** enough.

5. According to Millan, two lessons we can learn from dogs are **honesty** / **confidence** and integrity.

C Read the statements in the chart. Then write who Millan is talking about.

UNDERSTANDING PRONOUN REFERENCE

What Millan says directly in the reading	Who he is talking about
1. They have Harvard degrees, but they can't control a dog.	
2. They wanted me to be a professional, like a doctor or lawyer.	
3. They will never stab you in the back or lie to you.	

> **CRITICAL THINKING** When you make an **inference**, you conclude something based on things a person suggests *indirectly*, not what the person states *directly*.

D Read three possible inferences based on what Millan says in exercise C. Match each inference to one of the statements (1–3).

CRITICAL THINKING: INFERRING OPINION

_____ a. They didn't really like his job.

_____ b. In some ways, he likes them better than humans.

_____ c. They seem to find managing a dog an extremely difficult task.

DEVELOPING READING SKILLS

READING SKILL Recognizing Noun Clauses

A noun clause is a type of dependent (or subordinate) clause. Dependent clauses cannot stand alone as sentences; they are always part of a sentence.

A noun clause has a subject and a verb, and acts like a noun in a sentence.

$$\text{subject} \quad \text{verb}$$

*A dog doesn't know <u>how much **we spend** on it</u>.*
main clause   noun clause

To identify noun clauses …

1. Look for a subordinating conjunction—usually *that* or a *wh-* word—and the information it introduces.

   *Do you know <u>who **Cesar Millan is**</u>?*   (*Do you know <u>him</u>?*)
   *I don't know <u>how old **the dog is**</u>.*   (*I don't know <u>its age</u>.*)
   *I believe <u>that **she is** right</u>.*   (*I believe <u>her</u>.*)
   <u>*What **Millan says**</u> *makes sense to me.*   (*<u>He</u> makes sense to me.*)

2. Check that the clause has a subject and a verb. (See bold words in 1.)

3. Replace the clause with a noun or pronoun to check that the sentence makes sense. (See sentences in parentheses in 1.)

RECOGNIZING NOUN CLAUSES

A Match the noun clauses (a–c) to complete each sentence (1–3). Then scan the interview to check your answers.

1. A dog doesn't know _____
2. I see the dog, and I know _____
3. [My father] still can't understand _____

a. who you are.
b. that it lives in Beverly Hills.
c. why Americans pay me for walking their dogs.

RECOGNIZING NOUN CLAUSES

B Read the paragraph below. Find and underline five more noun clauses. Then note answers to the questions and discuss them with a partner.

Does your preference for dogs or cats say a lot about <u>who you are</u>? Sam Gosling, a psychologist at the University of Texas in Austin, decided to find out. In particular, Gosling wanted to learn what the characteristics of certain types of pet owners are. In the study, Gosling first found out how people classify themselves: as dog people, cat people, neither, or both. Then he gave the same people a standard personality test. The results showed what Gosling expected: dog people and cat people are different. For example, Gosling learned that dog people are more outgoing than cat people. Cat people are also generally more imaginative than dog people. Why these differences exist, however, is still a mystery.

1. What did Gosling want to learn in his study?   _____

2. What did Gosling find out first?   _____

3. What was one result of Gosling's study?   _____

Video

GORILLA TOOLMAKERS

A gorilla looks for food using a tree branch.

BEFORE VIEWING

A Work with a partner. In what ways do you think humans and gorillas are similar?

PREDICTING

Both humans and gorillas _____

_____

B Read the information below. Using the information and your own ideas, what do you think animals use tools for? Note some possible reasons. Then share your ideas with a partner.

LEARNING ABOUT THE TOPIC

Using a tool to solve problems is a sign of high intelligence. People once thought that humans were the only animals able to do this. However, scientists have discovered that a wide range of animals are actually able to work with tools. The American alligator, for example, has a unique way of catching its food. It waits in the water with sticks balanced on its head. Certain types of birds use these sticks to build their nests. When the birds come to collect the sticks, the alligator attacks!

1. _____

2. _____

3. _____

4. _____

C The words and phrases in **bold** below are used in the video. Read the sentences. Then match the correct form of each word or phrase to its definition.

River otters use **sticks** to build their homes along river banks.

There is **evidence** that humans and great apes share many similarities.

Humans **invented** robots to help with difficult tasks such as carrying heavy items.

Humans are one of the few animals able to **think through** problems and solve them in a creative way.

1. _____ (n) a thin piece of wood from a tree

2. _____ (v) to create something for the first time

3. _____ (n) information that shows something might be true

4. _____ (v) to consider something carefully until you understand it

WHILE VIEWING

A ▶ Watch the video. Which of the following statements describes what Breuer and Stokes's study discovered?

a   People can easily train gorillas to use tools.

b. Wild gorillas are able to use tools in ways never seen before.

c. Wild gorillas are better at using tools than gorillas in zoos.

B ▶ Watch the video again. Circle the correct answers.

1. Breuer was amazed when he saw Leah the gorilla using a tool **the same way humans do / she got from a human.**

2. Leah used a tool to **get fruit from a tree / check the depth of the water.**

3. Animals such as chimpanzees use tools that help them **find food / protect themselves.**

4. Breuer saw Efi the gorilla **using a new tool / communicating with another gorilla** to solve a problem.

AFTER VIEWING

A Work with a partner. How is gorilla behavior similar to, and different from, human behavior?

_____

_____

B Note your answers to the questions below. Then discuss with a partner.

How does studying animal behavior help us? What do you think we can learn from it?

_____

_____

Reading 2

PREPARING TO READ

A The words in **blue** below are used in the reading passage on pages 172–173. Complete the sentences using the correct words.

BUILDING VOCABULARY

> Someone who is **fair** treats everyone the same way.
>
> A **reward** is something you get for doing a good job.
>
> If you **expect** something, you think that it will happen.
>
> Being **willing** to help means you don't mind helping someone.
>
> Your **response** to something is what you do, think, or feel about it.
>
> If you **continue** to do something, you keep doing it without stopping.
>
> When people **cooperate**, they work together to achieve the same goal.
>
> **Research** involves studying something and trying to discover facts about it.

1. The law has to be _____ to everyone.

2. Some animals may not be _____ to share their food.

3. Dogs sometimes don't know when to stop eating. They often _____ to eat as long as they have food in front of them.

4. Ground squirrels live in groups. They _____ with one another by making a sound when they sense danger nearby.

5. Recent _____ on gorilla behavior shows that gorillas may be able to use tools.

6. Scientists didn't _____ gorillas in the wild to be able to use tools.

7. If you give a dog a(n) _____ for good behavior, it is likely to continue behaving well.

8. Anger is a normal _____ to unfair treatment.

B Discuss these questions with a partner.

USING VOCABULARY

1. Can you think of a time when you received treatment that was not **fair**?

2. What was your **response**?

C Read the main title and the headings on pages 172–173. What do you think the passage is about? Then check your answer as you read.

PREDICTING

a. how monkeys are helping humans

b. recent studies of monkey behavior

c. why monkeys are intelligent

DO MONKEYS HAVE FEELINGS?

🎧 18

MONKEYS SHOW A SENSE OF FAIRNESS

A Most humans **expect** to receive **fair** treatment. A scientific study shows that brown capuchin monkeys may feel the same way. This is the first time scientists have seen this kind of behavior in a species other than humans.

B Scientists chose brown capuchin monkeys for their **research** because they are known to have strong social bonds. In other words, capuchins have close relationships with each other. They also **cooperate**. For example, they share responsibilities for food-gathering activities, such as finding fruit trees.

C Sarah Brosnan, the leader of the study, put female monkeys in pairs. A different researcher worked with each pair of capuchins. The researchers trained the monkeys to give them a small rock. "That may sound simple, but not very many species are **willing** to [give things away]," says Brosnan. When a monkey exchanged a rock with the researcher within 60 seconds, it received a **reward**. Usually, the reward was a piece of cucumber.

D The partner of each capuchin who made an exchange also received a reward. Sometimes the partner got the same reward (a cucumber slice), but other times the partner received a better reward (a grape). Brosnan said the **response** to the unequal treatment was astonishing.[1] When a capuchin saw its partner get better treatment, it was unhappy. Some did not want to **continue** the test or eat the cucumber they received. Some threw their food at the researchers.

E Brosnan's research suggests there is a link between animal cooperation and a dislike of unfair treatment. This could have implications for discussions about equal treatment in human society. If animals are hardwired[2] to expect fair treatment, it's possible that we are, too.

[1] **astonishing:** very surprising
[2] **hardwired:** naturally behaving in a certain way

▼ Research suggests capuchin monkeys, such as this one in Costa Rica, care about fair treatment.

▲ Aside from humans, macaques are the most widespread type of primate. They live in places ranging from Japan (pictured) to North Africa.

"LOVE DRUG" RESULTS IN KINDER MONKEYS

F   Scientists studying monkeys found some surprising results using a chemical called oxytocin. Oxytocin is a hormone produced by humans and other mammals. It is sometimes called the "love hormone," because it is related to bonding and maternal behavior. Women produce large amounts of oxytocin during and after childbirth. Scientists believe this makes mothers feel more connected to their children.

G   The scientists at Duke University, in North Carolina, U.S.A., studied a monkey species called macaques. They wanted to see how the macaques responded to larger-than-normal amounts of oxytocin. In the experiment, some of the monkeys breathed in the hormone. Then they had to make a choice: drink a serving of fruit juice or give it to another monkey. The ones who got extra oxytocin were more likely to give their fruit juice to other monkeys. This may show that oxytocin improves social skills and makes individuals more aware of others.

UNDERSTANDING THE READING

UNDERSTANDING
MAIN IDEAS

A Match the main ideas (a–e) from *Monkeys Show a Sense of Fairness* to the correct category (1–5).

a. The monkeys got angry when they experienced unfair treatment.
b. Scientists gave unequal rewards to pairs of monkeys.
c. whether expectation of fair treatment is a natural human behavior
d. to find out if capuchin monkeys value fair treatment
e. There may be a link between animal cooperation and their dislike of unfair treatment.

1. Purpose of the study   _____
2. How researchers did the study   _____
3. What researchers noticed   _____
4. What researchers concluded   _____
5. Question for further research   _____

SUMMARIZING

B Complete the summary of *"Love Drug" Results in Kinder Monkeys.*

1. Scientists were interested to know if the hormone _____ would change the behavior of monkeys, so they tested this out on _____, a species of monkey.

2. During the experiment, the monkeys were given a choice: they could choose to _____ some juice, or give it to _____.

3. The experiment results showed that monkeys with more oxytocin were more likely to _____.

4. Scientists concluded that the "love hormone" made the monkeys _____.

UNDERSTANDING
PRONOUN
REFERENCE

C Find these sentences on pages 172–173. Then circle the noun that each underlined pronoun refers to. Check your answers with a partner.

1. Scientists chose brown capuchin monkeys for their research because <u>they</u> are known to have strong social bonds.

   a. capuchins   b. scientists

2. The researchers trained the monkeys to give <u>them</u> a small rock.

   a. other monkeys   b. the researchers

3. <u>They</u> wanted to see how the macaques responded to larger-than-normal amounts of oxytocin.

   a. the scientists   b. the macaques

CRITICAL THINKING:
APPLYING

D Work with a partner. How do you think humans would respond in an experiment similar to the one on the capuchins? Would people respond in a similar or different way?

Writing

EXPLORING WRITTEN ENGLISH

A Read the sentences. Write "S" if the sentence describes a similarity, and "D" if it describes a difference. Then underline the words in the sentences that show similarities and differences.

NOTICING

1. _____ Both chimpanzees and gorillas use tools.

2. _____ Unlike humans, dogs cannot solve complex problems.

3. _____ Giraffes eat plants. In contrast, lions eat meat.

4. _____ Like humans, gorillas solve problems by planning.

5. _____ Humans get angry if they are treated unfairly. Similarly, capuchin moneys do not like unequal treatment.

6. _____ Elephant seals are able to stay underwater for long periods of time. Humans, however, can't stay underwater for a long time without special equipment.

LANGUAGE FOR WRITING Making Comparisons

You can use the comparative form of adjectives to talk about similarities and differences between two things. You can also use other words and expressions for making comparisons.

Showing Similarities

> **Both** gorillas **and** chimpanzees use tools.
> **Like** gorillas, chimpanzees are endangered.
> Gorillas mainly eat plants. **Similarly**, monkeys are mostly herbivores.

- Use the plural form of the verb with the expression *both … and …* .

- Use a comma after the word *similarly*, and after an expression with *Like* … .

Showing Differences

> **Unlike** gorillas, monkeys have tails.
> Monkeys live about 30 years. **In contrast**, apes can live almost 60 years.
> Dogs are easily trained. **However**, it is very difficult to train a cat. / Dogs are easily trained. It is very difficult, **however**, to train a cat.

- Use a comma after the word *however* and after expressions with *Unlike* … and *In contrast* … . Refer to the sentences above for the position of the comma.

- If *however* is in the middle of a sentence, add a comma before and after it.

B Use the words or phrases in the parentheses to link the sentences (1–5).

1. Humans can make tools. Dogs cannot make tools. (*unlike*)

   _____

2. Apes eat insects. Bats eat insects. (*both … and*)

   _____

3. Reptiles lay eggs. Mammals give birth to live babies. (*in contrast*)

   _____

4. Capuchins live in the Western Hemisphere. Macaques live in the Eastern Hemisphere. (*however*)

   _____

   _____

5. German shepherds can become guide dogs. Capuchin monkeys can be trained to help people. (*similarly*)

   _____

   _____

C Look at the Venn diagram of two dog breeds. Use your dictionary to look up any words you don't know.

Australian Terrier
can be aggressive
has long hair
lives 12–14 years
barks a lot

alert
social
good with children
easy to train

Basenji
calm
has short hair
lives 10–12 years
doesn't bark much

Discuss with a partner: How are Australian Terriers and Basenjis similar? How are they different?

Write sentences using the words and phrases below.

Both … and … *Similarly, …* *However, …*
Like … , *Unlike … ,* *In contrast, …*

_____

_____

_____

_____

In a comparison paragraph, you normally focus on either similarities or differences. Each supporting idea in this kind of paragraph describes a similarity or a difference about the two things that you're comparing. The detail sentences give examples to explain each similarity or difference. The structure generally looks like this:

1. topic sentence (state the two items you are comparing or contrasting)
2. supporting idea 1 (name a similarity or difference, e.g., in size, color, or behavior)
3. detail 1 (provide an example or more information)
4. supporting idea 2
5. detail 2
6. supporting idea 3
7. detail 3

D Form a comparison paragraph by putting the sentences below in order (1–7).   SEQUENCING

_____ a. Lastly, the two animals share the same conservation status.

_____ b. Both are found in the wild throughout Africa and parts of Asia.

_____ c. First of all, they look similar.

___1___ d. Leopards and cheetahs share a number of similarities.

_____ e. Secondly, they live in similar regions of the world.

_____ f. They are listed as "vulnerable" by the IUCN (International Union for Conservation of Nature).

_____ g. Both are large, cat-like animals with a spotted pattern on their fur.

E Read the paragraph below. Then write a suitable topic sentence for it.   WRITING A TOPIC SENTENCE

Firstly, while leopards and cheetahs look similar, it's quite easy to tell them apart. Cheetahs are much slimmer than leopards, and the markings on their fur are quite different. **Also**, cheetahs are much faster. Leopards can reach speeds of around 60 km/h over a short distance, but cheetahs are known to reach around 120 km/h. **Lastly**, their hunting behavior is different. Leopards usually hunt at night and move quietly to surprise their prey. Cheetahs, **however**, hunt during the day or night and use their great speed to chase down other animals.

Topic sentence: _____

_____

F Match the **bold** words in the paragraph above to words that have a similar meaning.

_____ 1. Firstly   a. Finally

_____ 2. Also   b. To begin with

_____ 3. Lastly   c. In contrast

_____ 4. However   d. What's more

WRITING TASK

GOAL You are going to write a paragraph about the following topic:

Compare the behavior of two kinds of animals.

BRAINSTORMING **A** Make a list of three to four animals that you are familiar with. Use the ones you read about in this unit or your own ideas. Next to each one, make notes on what you know about its behavior.

Example: *Gorilla: uses tools   can walk on two legs   uses instinct   uses thumbs*

PLANNING **B** Follow these steps to make notes for your paragraph. Don't worry about grammar or spelling. Don't write complete sentences.

Step 1 Look at your notes from exercise A. Choose two animals that you want to compare. Decide whether you want to write about their similarities or differences.

Step 2 List at least three types of behavior (either similarities or differences) in the outline and note them as your supporting ideas.

Step 3 Include at least one detail for each supporting idea.

Step 4 Write a topic sentence that tells the reader what you are going to discuss in the paragraph.

OUTLINE

Topic sentence: _____

_____

Supporting Idea 1: _____

_____

Detail: _____

_____

Supporting Idea 2: _____

_____

Detail: _____

_____

Supporting Idea 3: _____

_____

Detail: _____

_____

FIRST DRAFT **C** Use the information in your outline to write a first draft of your paragraph.

REVISING PRACTICE

The drafts below are similar to the one you are going to write.

What did the writer do in Draft 2 to improve the paragraph? Match the changes (a–d) to the highlighted parts.

a. added a detail to a supporting idea
b. corrected language for making comparisons
c. improved the topic sentence
d. deleted unrelated information

Draft 1

There are two main species of gorilla—the western gorilla and the eastern gorilla. They are a little different. First of all, as their names suggest, they live in separate parts of Africa. Secondly, though both animals are huge, western gorillas are slightly small than eastern gorillas. Western gorillas weigh up to about 180 kilograms, while the weight of eastern gorillas can be up to 220 kilograms. Finally, the hair on the gorillas' bodies differs slightly. Eastern gorillas have darker and longer hair, especially on their arms, which they use when they walk.

Draft 2

There are two main species of gorilla—the western gorilla and the eastern gorilla. While they are very similar, there are a few ways in which they are different. First of all, as their names suggest, they live in separate parts of Africa. Their habitats are about 900 kilometers apart. Secondly, though both animals are huge, western gorillas are slightly smaller than eastern gorillas. Western gorillas weigh up to about 180 kilograms, while the weight of eastern gorillas can be up to 220 kilograms. Finally, the hair on the gorillas' bodies differs slightly. Eastern gorillas have darker and longer hair, especially on their arms.

☐
☐
☐
☐

D Now use the questions below to revise your paragraph.

REVISED DRAFT

☐ Did you include a topic sentence?

☐ Did you include three supporting ideas?

☐ Did you include at least one detail for each supporting idea?

☐ Did you use language for making comparisons correctly?

☐ Do all your sentences relate to the main idea?

EDITING PRACTICE

Read the information below.

In sentences with comparison words and expressions, remember to:
- use the plural form of the verb with *both . . . and*.
- use *similarly* and *in contrast* at the start of a sentence, and follow them with a comma.
- use *like* and *unlike* with a noun or a noun phrase followed by a comma.
- use a comma after *however* when it is at the start of a sentence.
- use a comma before and after *however* when it is in the middle of a sentence.

Correct one mistake with comparison words and expressions in each of the sentences (1–8).

1. Like humans do, chimpanzees use tools to solve problems.

2. Both female capuchins and humans values fairness.

3. Some chimpanzees use tools in zoos. To contrast, gorillas rarely use tools in captivity.

4. Unlike cats need, dogs need a lot of attention from their owners.

5. Some dog trainers believe in punishing bad behavior. However other trainers believe in rewarding good behavior.

6. Both Basenjis and Australian Terriers makes good pets for children.

7. Scientists often use monkeys in behavioral studies. Similarly rats are useful for scientific research on behavior.

8. Like children dogs need a lot of training and attention.

FINAL DRAFT **E** Follow these steps to write a final draft.

1. Check your revised draft for mistakes with words and expressions for making comparisons.
2. Now use the checklist on page 218 to write a final draft. Make any other necessary changes.

UNIT REVIEW

Answer the following questions.

1. Besides tool use, what are some other examples that show animals' intelligence?

_____

_____

_____

2. What are some words that introduce noun clauses?

_____

_____

_____

3. Do you remember the meanings of these words? Check (✓) the ones you know. Look back at the unit and review the ones you don't know.

Reading 1:
- ☐ angry
- ☐ approach AWL
- ☐ companion
- ☐ confused
- ☐ owner
- ☐ pet
- ☐ powerful
- ☐ profession
- ☐ trainer
- ☐ work out

Reading 2:
- ☐ continue
- ☐ cooperate AWL
- ☐ expect
- ☐ fair
- ☐ research AWL
- ☐ response AWL
- ☐ reward
- ☐ willing

THE POWER OF IMAGES

10

Usain Bolt competing at the 2016 Olympics,
taken by photographer Cameron Spencer

THINK AND DISCUSS

1 In your opinion, what makes a photograph powerful?
2 Describe a photograph you like. Why do you like it?

181

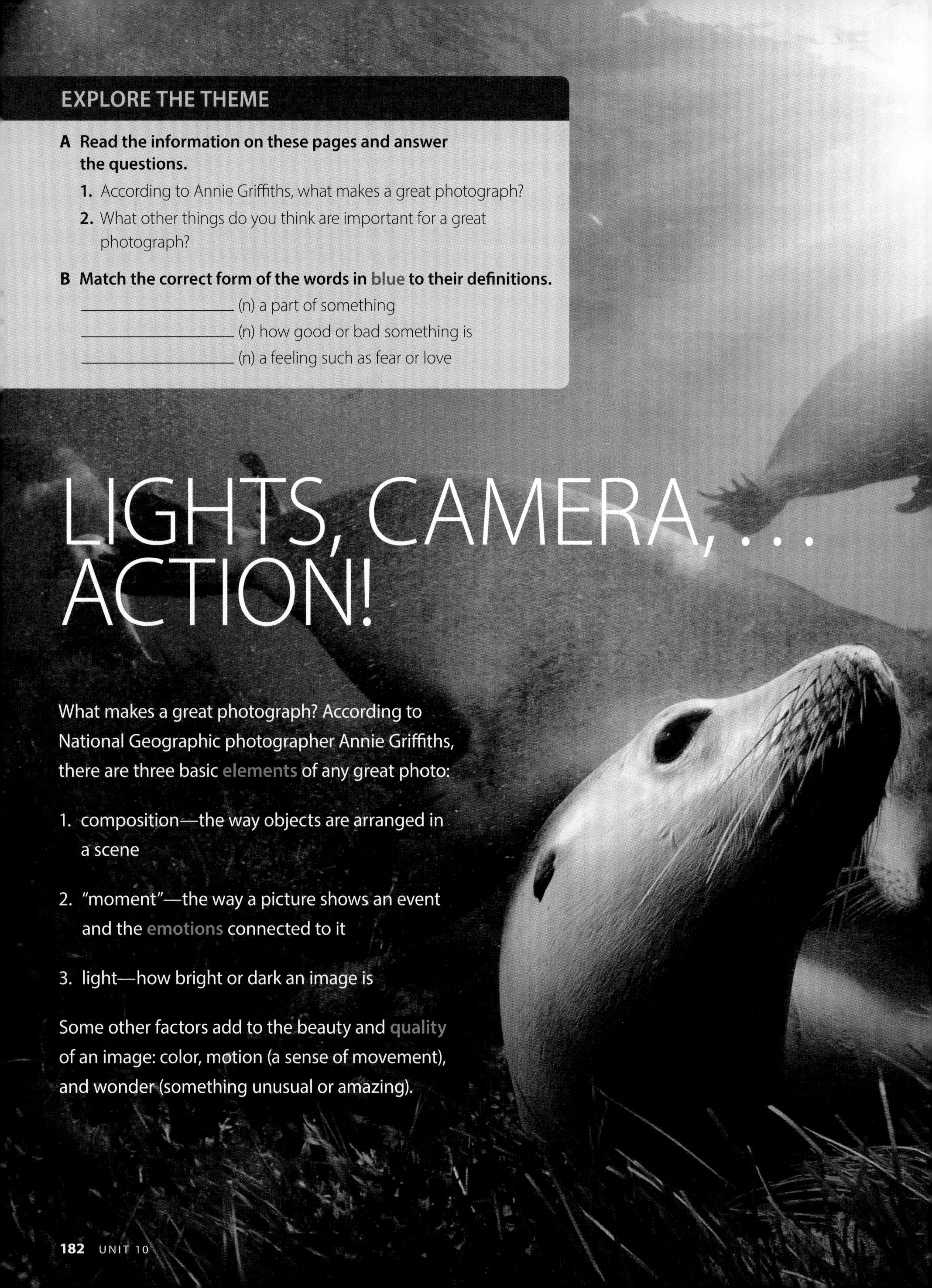

A Read the information on these pages and answer the questions.

1. According to Annie Griffiths, what makes a great photograph?

2. What other things do you think are important for a great photograph?

B Match the correct form of the words in blue to their definitions.

_____ (n) a part of something

_____ (n) how good or bad something is

_____ (n) a feeling such as fear or love

LIGHTS, CAMERA, . . . ACTION!

What makes a great photograph? According to National Geographic photographer Annie Griffiths, there are three basic elements of any great photo:

1. composition—the way objects are arranged in a scene

2. "moment"—the way a picture shows an event and the emotions connected to it

3. light—how bright or dark an image is

Some other factors add to the beauty and quality of an image: color, motion (a sense of movement), and wonder (something unusual or amazing).

1. Photographer David Doubilet took this photo of sea lions playing in the water off the coast of South Australia.

2. Jim Blair took this picture in Dacca, Bangladesh. It shows a moment of joy as one boy jumps off the back of a water buffalo.

3. Danish photographer Sisse Brimberg took this picture in a park in Russia. It shows a universal experience—a mother's pride in her child.

Reading 1

PREPARING TO READ

BUILDING VOCABULARY

A The words in **blue** below are used in the reading passage on pages 185–188. Read the sentences. Then match the correct form of each word or phrase to its definition.

> David Doubilet's photo shows a **scene** of sea lions playing in the water.
>
> People often hire professional photographers for an important **ceremony**, such as a wedding.
>
> Photographer Jim Blair was walking across a bridge when **suddenly** he spotted a boy jumping off the back of a water buffalo.
>
> Photography is a form of **visual** art, like painting or sculpture.
>
> Brimberg's photo **captures** a special moment between a mother and her baby.
>
> Annie Griffiths **points out** that a great photo has to have three basic elements.
>
> Photographs can **remind** you of important events in your life.

1. _____ (adv) happening quickly and unexpectedly

2. _____ (n) a type of formal event

3. _____ (v) to show or tell someone about something

4. _____ (adj) used to describe something you can see

5. _____ (v) to make you think about something again

6. _____ (v) to record an event in a movie or a photograph

7. _____ (n) a view that you see in a picture

USING VOCABULARY

B Discuss these questions with a partner.

1. What kinds of things do people usually **capture** in photos?
2. How do you **remind** yourself about important things?

BRAINSTORMING

C Work with a partner. Discuss your answers to this question:

What emotions can photos show? Give three examples.

1. _____   2. _____   3. _____

PREDICTING

D Look at the three main photos on pages 186–188. What do you think is happening in each one? Discuss with a partner. Then check your ideas as you read the passage.

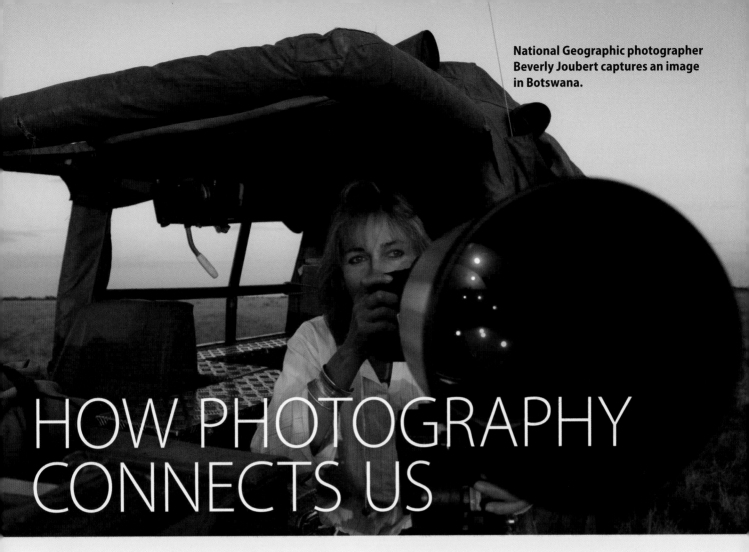

National Geographic photographer Beverly Joubert captures an image in Botswana.

HOW PHOTOGRAPHY CONNECTS US

🎧 19

A   One day some years ago, David Griffin was at a beach watching his son swimming in the water. Suddenly, a big wave caught the boy and started to pull him out to sea. As Griffin ran to help his son, time seemed to slow down. The scene froze. Griffin can still remember what the moment felt like. "There's a wave about to crash onto him," he says. "I can see his hands reaching out, and I can see his face in terror, looking at me, saying, 'Help me, Dad.'"

B   Griffin was able to help his son out of the water and both were fine. But Griffin will never forget the details of the event. For Griffin, it is an example of a "flashbulb[1] memory." In a flashbulb memory, all the elements of an event come together. These elements include both the event and the viewer's emotions as the event is happening. In these situations, time slows down and details become very clear.

C   Today, Griffin is an award-winning photography director. He believes that a great photograph is like a flashbulb memory. It copies the way the mind works when something important is happening. It shows the event, and also the story and feelings behind the event. "I believe that photography can make a real connection to people," says Griffin. In other words, we do not just see the event in a photo. We also feel an emotional connection with it.

[1] A **flashbulb** is a lightbulb attached to a camera. It lights up a scene for a very short period of time.

The best professional photojournalists, says Griffin, "create a **visual**
D narrative." That is, they know how to use pictures to tell a story. Here are
some examples.

The 2007 photo above by Brent Stirton features a 225-kilogram
silverback gorilla called Senkwekwe. Several gorillas were killed illegally that
E year. The photo shows villagers carrying Senkwekwe from Virunga Park in
the Democratic Republic of Congo (DRC) to a special burial place.

The photo had a powerful impact around the world. People became
more aware of the dangers facing wild animals. "This photograph changed
F everything for me," Stirton said. "[It] got a much bigger response than anything
that I'd shot before to do with people. The gorillas were seen as true innocents."

In 2005, Randy Olson traveled to central Africa's Ituri Forest for a photo story. His goal was to photograph a pygmy tribe called the Mbuti. Pygmies are some of the shortest people in the world—most adult males are less than 4 feet 11 inches (150 centimeters) tall. They are also very difficult to reach, as they live deep inside the forest. In the foreground[2] of the image below is a blind, young Mbuti boy. He is getting ready for a **ceremony** to mark the beginning of his life as an adult. Behind him is a young Mbuti girl. "I love this photograph because it **reminds** me of Degas's bronze sculptures of a little dancer," says Griffin.

▲ **Statue of a ballet dancer, by Edgar Degas**

G

[2] The **foreground** of an image is the area in the front.

The image above was taken in 2016 by amateur[3] photographer Son Truong. He photographed a woman in the Vietnamese countryside working while her daughter played on a swing. Although many of the most powerful images are taken by professional photographers, Griffin **points out** that amateur photographers can also **capture** a special moment. "The **quality** of amateur photographs can at times be amazing," he says. "Everyone has at least one, maybe two, great photos in them."

H

[3]If you are an **amateur**, you do something as a hobby and not as a job.

UNDERSTANDING THE READING

A Look back at page 185 to answer these questions.

Look back at page 185

UNDERSTANDING
MAIN IDEAS

1. What personal event does Griffin describe?

_____

2. What is a flashbulb memory?

_____

3. Why does Griffin think a great photo is like a flashbulb memory?

_____

B Which image(s) does each description (a–f) refer to? Some items are used more than once.

UNDERSTANDING
DETAILS

a. was taken in Africa
b. shows a sad event
c. was taken by an amateur photographer

d. features two people as the main subjects
e. reminds Griffin of a famous piece of art
f. raised awareness of a conservation issue

1. gorilla   _____

2. pygmy ceremony   _____

3. Vietnamese family   _____

> **CRITICAL THINKING** Sometimes you can **evaluate** something using a set of criteria (factors). For example, when deciding how good a photograph is, you could consider things like the composition or lighting.

C Refer back to Annie Griffiths' ideas on the three elements necessary for a great photograph on page 182. Use the criteria to rate the photos. (1 = lowest score; 5 = highest score)

Refer back to Annie Griffiths' ideas on the three elements necessary for a great photograph on page 182.

CRITICAL THINKING:
EVALUATING
USING CRITERIA

Photo	Composition	Moment	Light
gorilla			
pygmy ceremony			
Vietnamese family			

D Work with a partner. Is there another photo in this book that has an emotional connection for you? What emotions does it communicate?

CRITICAL THINKING:
ANALYZING

Description of photo: _____

Emotion(s) it communicates: _____

_____

DEVELOPING READING SKILLS

READING SKILL Identifying Subordinating Conjunctions

Subordinating conjunctions show relationships between ideas in clauses.

The subordinating conjunctions *after, before, until, while,* and *as* can show time relationships:

> <u>I decided to study photography</u> **after** <u>I saw Brent Stirton's photographs</u>.
>   independent clause   dependent clause

The subordinating conjunctions *although, even though, though,* and *while* can show contrast:

> **Although** <u>the camera was old</u>, <u>it took excellent pictures</u>.
>   dependent clause   independent clause

A comma comes at the end of an independent clause if the subordinating conjunction that follows is introducing a contrast.

> *I like taking photos of nature, while my sister prefers taking portraits of people.*

IDENTIFYING CONJUNCTIONS

A Read the sentences below. What kind of information does each underlined subordinating conjunction introduce? Write T for *time* and C for *contrast*.

_____ 1. Griffin ran to help his son <u>after</u> a big wave pulled the boy to sea.

_____ 2. Truong is an amateur photographer, <u>while</u> Stirton is a professional.

_____ 3. Griffin spoke about the photographs <u>while</u> showing them to an audience.

_____ 4. You usually cannot become a professional photographer <u>until</u> you have many years of experience.

_____ 5. <u>Although</u> the photo of the dead gorilla made many people sad, it made them aware of an environmental issue.

ANALYZING

B Find three sentences on pages 185–188 with subordinating conjunctions. Write the sentences and underline the conjunction(s). What does each one show? Circle **Time** or **Contrast**.

1. Paragraph A: _____

_____ **Time / Contrast**

2. Paragraph H: _____

_____ **Time / Contrast**

3. Paragraph H: _____

_____ **Time / Contrast**

APPLYING

C Choose two of the photographs from pages 185–188. Write a sentence about each one using a subordinating conjunction.

_____

_____

Video

PHOTO CAMP

Participants of the 2012
Photo Camp in the Bahamas

BEFORE VIEWING

A Look at the title of the video and read the photo caption. Who do you think attends this photo camp? What is its purpose?

PREDICTING

B Read the information about Photo Camp. Then circle the correct answers.

LEARNING ABOUT
THE TOPIC

At National Geographic Photo Camp, young people from all over the world can learn how to take pictures. But this project doesn't just teach people how to take good photos. Its goal is to give children in difficult situations a way to tell their own stories. As the camp director Kirsten Elstner explains, "Photo Camp is about storytelling. We're focused on using the camera to see things and to tell a story." Since 2003, Photo Camp has taken place in over 70 different places and worked with over 1,500 young people. The participants live in refugee[1] camps, Native American reservations, and inner city neighborhoods in locations like New York and Washington, D.C.

[1]**Refugees** are people who have to leave their homes, usually due to war or a natural disaster.

1. National Geographic Photo Camp works mainly with **young** / **elderly** people.

2. Photo Camp wants to help people **tell their stories** / **make new friends** through photography.

3. The location of Photo Camp **is** / **isn't** always the same.

4. The people who join the camp are usually **people in difficult situations** / **photography students**.

C The words in **bold** below are used in the video. Read the paragraph. Then match the correct form of each word to its definition.

In 2015, National Geographic photographer Reza Deghati organized a huge photo **exhibition** in Paris. His photos covered the walls along the banks of the River Seine. The **temporary** exhibition, which lasted for twelve weeks, featured **portraits** of refugees from around the world. The aim was to **document** the experiences of refugees and raise awareness of the difficulties they face.

1. _____ (v) to make a record of something

2. _____ (n) a picture of a person

3. _____ (n) an event where people come to see art

4. _____ (adj) lasting for only a limited amount of time

WHILE VIEWING

UNDERSTANDING
MAIN IDEAS

A ▶ Watch the video. Check (✓) the benefits of Photo Camp.

☐ 1. The students can learn how to take photos.

☐ 2. Photo Camp helps to raise money for refugees.

☐ 3. Some students will be able to use their new skill in their future life.

☐ 4. The photos that students take are published in a magazine.

UNDERSTANDING
DETAILS

B ▶ Watch the video again. Circle T for *true* or F for *false*.

1. The students haven't used cameras before.	T	F
2. The students at Photo Camp are all from Uganda.	T	F
3. Aganze Grace is a professional photographer.	T	F
4. The students show what they've learned in Photo Camp through an exhibition.	T	F

AFTER VIEWING

REACTING TO
THE VIDEO

A Discuss these questions with a partner.

1. Reza Deghati says he "uses photography like language." What do you think he means?
2. Besides refugees, what other groups of people do you think Photo Camp could include?

CRITICAL THINKING:
APPLYING

B Work with a partner. If you were organizing a photo camp, what group of people would it be for? Where would you hold it and what would its goal be?

Target participants: _____

Place: _____

Goal(s) of camp: _____

_____

Reading 2

PREPARING TO READ

A The words and phrases in **blue** below are used in the reading passage on pages 194–195. Complete each sentence with the correct word or phrase.

BUILDING VOCABULARY

> If an item **belongs** to you, you own it.
>
> A **frightened** person is afraid, anxious, or nervous.
>
> If something is **incredible**, it is very good or very surprising.
>
> A **calm** person does not feel much worry, fear, or excitement.
>
> If something happens **immediately**, it happens very quickly.
>
> A **relationship** is a connection between two or more people or things.
>
> If something is true **according to** someone, the information comes from that person.
>
> If you are **disappointed**, you are sad because something is not as good as you hoped.

1. Photographers feel _____ if they miss a great moment to take a shot.

2. _____ David Griffin, the best photographs make an emotional connection.

3. It can be difficult to remain _____ when you're in a dangerous situation.

4. Brimberg's photo shows the close _____ between a mother and her child.

5. Although the young refugees at Photo Camp are amateur photographers, the photos they took were _____ .

6. David Griffin was _____ when he saw his son caught in a big wave.

7. Digital cameras allow people to view a photo _____ after they take it.

8. You need to ask photographers for permission before using a photo that _____ to them.

B Discuss these questions with a partner.

USING VOCABULARY

1. When you feel nervous, what do you do to stay **calm**?

2. In what kinds of situations do you feel **frightened**?

C Look at the photos on pages 194–195 and skim the first two paragraphs. What was the purpose of Nicklen's visit to Antarctica? What do you think happened?

PREDICTING

A VERY CLOSE ENCOUNTER

 20

A   Imagine looking straight into these jaws! They **belong** to a leopard seal, one of the top predators[1] in the waters of the Antarctic. A leopard seal's front teeth are sharp enough to tear apart its prey[2] in seconds. Usually, the seal hunts fish, squid, and penguins. **According to** scientists, leopard seals rarely attack humans.

B   The man behind the camera is National Geographic photographer Paul Nicklen. Nicklen has spent much of his life exploring polar regions. He is passionate[3] about protecting these cold environments and the animals that live there. He is especially interested in leopard seals. "Are they really so dangerous?" Nicklen wondered. So he decided to travel to Antarctica to find out. Here is his story.

[1]**Predators** are animals that kill and eat other animals.
[2]An animal's **prey** are the animals that it hunts and eats.
[3]If a person is **passionate** about something, they have very strong feelings about it.

The seal brings Nicklen a penguin.

Adult leopard seals can grow to a length of about 3.6 meters, and weigh as much as 450 kilograms.

C "One day, I was standing on the boat when a very large female leopard seal swam by. I put on my diving gear and got my camera. I was **frightened** because she was so big. My mouth was dry. At first, I couldn't even move. But I knew it was time to get closer to this mysterious creature.

D I jumped into the freezing water. **Immediately**, the seal swam toward me. Then she put my entire camera—and much of my head—into her mouth. Thinking this must be a threat[4] display, I decided to stay very **calm**.

E Although the seal was showing me her teeth, I tried not to show any fear. She did it a few more times, scratching up my camera, and then swam away. Then she came back with a live penguin. The penguin was meant for me to eat. Of course, I didn't eat the penguin, and I think the seal was very **disappointed**.

F I realized the seal thought I was another large predator. The two most important things in a leopard seal's life are eating and breeding.[5] So perhaps this seal was worried about me—she didn't want me to starve. She brought me several penguins. She even tried to show me how to eat them. The seal tried to push penguins into my camera—she thought the camera was my mouth!

G As a biologist, I understood that she was trying to feed me. But I think that she was really trying to communicate with me. At this point, she didn't seem very dangerous. She stayed by me and tried to feed me for four days. One time, she noticed another leopard seal come up behind me. She made a deep, threatening sound and scared the other seal away. She then took that seal's penguin and gave it to me.

H Those four days were the most **incredible** experience I ever had as a wildlife photographer. I got some amazing pictures. I also learned that animals do not always behave the way we expect. My **relationship** with this powerful and intelligent animal will stay with me forever."

[4] A **threat** is a way of showing the intention to do harm.
[5] **Breeding** means having babies.

UNDERSTANDING THE READING

UNDERSTANDING
MAIN IDEAS

A Choose the best alternative title for the reading passage.

    a. Protecting Antarctic Animals

    b. How Leopard Seals Hunt

    c. An Unforgettable Experience

SEQUENCING

B Put the events in Nicklen's story in the order they happened (1–8).

    _____ a. Nicklen put on his gear and got into the water.

    _____ b. A leopard seal swam by Nicklen's boat.

    _____ c. The seal tried to give Nicklen a penguin to eat.

    _____ d. The seal put Nicklen's camera and head into her mouth.

    __4__ e. The seal swam toward Nicklen as soon as he got into the water.

    _____ f. Nicklen went to Antarctica to photograph leopard seals.

    _____ g. The seal stayed with Nicklen, and she protected him for four days.

    _____ h. Nicklen didn't eat the penguin, and the seal seemed disappointed.

PARAPHRASING

C Work with a partner. Take turns retelling Nicklen's story to a partner using your own words. Include subordinating conjunctions (*although*, *after*, etc.) where appropriate.

CRITICAL THINKING:
EVALUATING
USING CRITERIA

D Work with a partner. Evaluate the photos in the reading using the elements of photography described on page 182. Which element do you think each photo illustrates best? Discuss the reasons for your choices.

light	composition	moment	color	motion	wonder

1. Element:

_____

Reason:

_____

_____

2. Element:

_____

Reason:

_____

_____

3. Element:

_____

Reason:

_____

_____

Writing

EXPLORING WRITTEN ENGLISH

LANGUAGE FOR WRITING Describing Spatial Relationships

You can use these phrases to describe images:

The image shows … / In this image, we [can] see …

In this image, we see a mother looking proudly at her baby.

You can also describe where things in the image are located:

behind	*next to / beside*
on the left / right	*in the middle (of)*
to the left / right (of)	*between X and Y*
in front of	*in the foreground / background (of)*

In the foreground, *we can see a boy getting ready for a ceremony.* **Behind** *him, there is a little girl in a grass skirt.*

In the photo, the girl is standing **to the right of** *the boy. We can see her standing* **between** *the boy and a tree.*

A Read the information in the Language for Writing box above. Then look at the photo of the mother and baby on page 183 and complete the sentences (1–8).

ANALYZING

Example: There is a hole in the ground (in front) / **in the middle** of the trees.

1. In the **background** / **foreground** of the image, there are several trees.

2. The mother is **behind** / **to the right of** the baby.

3. The baby is in the **front** / **back** of the scene.

4. The mother is on the **right** / **left** side of the photo.

5. The baby is **next to** / **in front of** the trees.

6. There are two trees **between** / **behind** the baby and the mother.

7. A man is sitting to the **right** / **left** of the hole in the ground.

8. The mother is in the **foreground** / **background** of the scene.

When you describe a picture, you can use adjectives to express sensory experiences—how people or things in the image look and feel:

> The people in the photo **seem joyful**.
>
> The scene **feels very sad**.
>
> The man **looks bored**.

In these cases, the adjectives follow the verbs *seem*, *feel*, and *look*.

You can also describe how an image makes you feel, or what it makes you think about:

> The image **makes** *us/me/people/the viewer feel* …
>
> It **makes** *us/me/people think of* …
>
> The girl in the Mbuti ceremony photo **reminds** *Griffin of a Degas sculpture*.

Notice that an object follows *remind* and *make*.

B Unscramble the words to make sentences that describe feelings and thoughts.

Example: of / me / light / the / water / the / on / think / makes / diamonds

The light on the water makes me think of diamonds.

1. and / happy / the / seems / relaxed / boy

   _____

2. angry / the / me / dead / and / sad / makes / gorilla / feel

   _____

3. look / a / the / clouds / house / like

   _____

4. of / reminds / problems / this / people / image / environmental

   _____

5. us / girl / of / young / the / famous / makes / sculpture / think / a

   _____

C Describe a photo in this unit using words and phrases for describing locations and feelings. Write your sentences below. Then read them to a partner. Can your partner guess which photo you are describing?

Description: _____

_____

How it makes me feel / What it makes me think of: _____

_____

_____

WRITING SKILL Writing an Opinion Paragraph

In an opinion paragraph, your topic sentence states your opinion:

Sisse Brimberg's image of a mother and her baby is an example of a great photograph.

Your supporting ideas give reasons for your opinion:

One reason the photo is great is because the colors are very beautiful.

Details can include examples or explanations:

For example, the green grass contrasts with the bright pink baby carriage and the mother's red hair. This makes the different colors in the photo stand out.

D Read this paragraph about the photograph below. Label the parts of the paragraph with the items (a–f):

a. the topic sentence
b. the concluding sentence
c. the first reason for the main idea
d. another reason for the main idea
e. details or explanation for the first reason
f. details or explanation for the second reason

This picture of trees in a snowstorm is a great photo. One reason the photo is great is because it has the element of motion. This makes the scene look very real. A heavy wind is blowing, and the trees are bending to the right. The wind is moving so fast that some of the tree branches are blurred. This blurring really gives the feeling of motion. Another thing that makes this photo great is the way it shows a moment in time. It makes a moving scene in nature stand still for a second, so we can see how powerful the storm is. In fact, the moment is so powerful that you feel you are also in the storm!

The Moment
by Peter Essick

WRITING TASK

GOAL You are going to write a paragraph on the following topic:

Describe a photograph and explain why you think it is an example of good photography.

BRAINSTORMING **A** Find three photographs that you think are great. You can use photos from this book, photos you find online, or your own photos. Discuss with a partner what makes each one good. Take notes on your ideas.

PLANNING **B** Follow these steps to make notes for your paragraph. Don't worry about grammar or spelling. Don't write complete sentences.

Step 1 Look at your brainstorming ideas in exercise A. Choose the one photo that you will write about.

Step 2 Write a topic sentence that expresses your opinion about the photo.

Step 3 Now choose three reasons for your choice and note them in the outline as your supporting ideas. Think about the elements of a great photo that you read about in this unit.

Step 4 Include one or two details in the outline to explain each supporting idea. Think about details that describe spatial relationships and emotions.

OUTLINE

Topic sentence: _____

_____

Supporting Idea 1: _____

_____

Detail: _____

Supporting Idea 2: _____

_____

Detail: _____

Supporting Idea 3: _____

_____

Detail: _____

FIRST DRAFT **C** Use the information in your outline to write a first draft of your paragraph.

REVISING PRACTICE

The drafts below are similar to the one you are going to write.

What did the writer do in Draft 2 to improve the paragraph? Match the changes (a–e) to the highlighted parts.

a. added a missing detail
b. added a topic sentence
c. improved the introduction of a supporting idea
d. corrected an error with describing emotions
e. corrected an error with describing spatial relationships

Draft 1

One reason Sisse Brimberg's photo is great is because of the colors the photographer captured. The photo's composition makes it great. The baby is in the middle of the scene, slightly behind in the left of the mother. Usually, in photos of mothers with their children, the main subjects are in the center of the photo. Finally, the picture is a good example of a moment in time and the emotions connected to it. The mother in the photo seem happy and proud of her baby. In summary, because of the use of color, the composition, and the emotion it captures, this is a great photo.

Draft 2

Sisse Brimberg's image of a mother and her baby is an example of a great photograph. One reason the photo is great is because of the colors the photographer captured. For example, the green grass contrasts with the bright pink baby carriage and the mother's red hair. The photo's composition is another thing that makes it great. The baby is in the middle of the scene, slightly behind and to the left of the mother. Usually, in photos of mothers with their children, the main subjects are in the center of the photo. Finally, the picture is a good example of a moment in time and the emotions connected to it. The mother in the photo seems happy and proud of her baby. In summary, because of the use of color, the composition, and the emotion it captures, this is a great photo.

□

□

□

□

□

D Now use the questions below to revise your paragraph.

REVISED DRAFT

□ Did you include a topic sentence that expresses an opinion?

□ Are your supporting ideas clear?

□ Did you include at least one detail to explain each supporting idea?

□ Did you accurately describe spatial relationships and emotions in the photo?

EDITING PRACTICE

Read the information below.

In sentences with phrases that describe location, remember to:

• use the correct words, for example, *between x* **and** *y* (not *between x* **to** *y*).

• be careful with words that have similar spelling, for example, *behind* and *beside*.

Correct one mistake with phrases that describe location in each of the sentences (1–8).

1. Next of the boys is a large group of elephants.

2. In this photo, a mother is sitting between her son to her daughter.

3. A young girl in a pink coat is standing behind of her brother.

4. At the middle of the scene, there is a small yellow fish.

5. Of the foreground, we see a small dog in a green sweater.

6. There is a large tree at behind the little boy.

7. There is a baby the right of her mother.

8. The children are beside to the water buffaloes.

FINAL DRAFT **E** Follow these steps to write a final draft.

1. Check your revised draft for mistakes with describing spatial relationships.

2. Now use the checklist on page 218 to write a final draft. Make any other necessary changes.

UNIT REVIEW

Answer the following questions.

1. Which photo in this unit do you think is most interesting? Why?

_____

_____

_____

2. What are two types of relationships that subordinating conjunctions can show?

_____

_____

_____

3. Do you remember the meanings of these words? Check (✔) the ones you know. Look back at the unit and review the ones you don't know.

Reading 1:

☐ capture   ☐ ceremony   ☐ element AWL

☐ emotion   ☐ point out   ☐ quality

☐ remind   ☐ scene   ☐ suddenly

☐ visual AWL

Reading 2:

☐ according to   ☐ belong   ☐ calm

☐ disappointed   ☐ frightened   ☐ immediately

☐ incredible   ☐ relationship

VOCABULARY EXTENSION   UNIT 1

WORD FORMS Verbs and Nouns

Some verbs ending in -t and -s can be made into nouns by adding -ion to the end of the word. For verbs ending in -e, spell the noun without the -e.

VERB	NOUN
communicate	communication
connect	connection
discuss	discussion

A Complete each sentence with the correct verb or noun form of the words below.

> communicate   connect   contribute   discuss   populate

1. We should have a meeting to _____ our project.

2. The _____ of the Earth is now over seven billion people.

3. Today, text messaging is one of the most popular forms of _____.

4. Anyone can upload a video to YouTube as long as they have an Internet _____.

5. To make the *Life in a Day* movie, the team asked people to _____ a video of their daily life.

WORD PARTNERS verb + *time*

Collocations are words that often go together, such as *spend time*. Some collocations are in the verb + noun form. Below are definitions for common collocations with the noun *time*.

have time: to be free to do something

spend time: to use time to do something

waste time: to use time without purpose

save time: to reduce the amount of time it takes to do something

kill time: to do something while waiting for something else to happen

B Complete each sentence with the correct form of the collocations from the box above.

1. The deadline for this project is tomorrow, so we can't _____ chatting.

2. I am really busy at the moment, so I don't _____ to take on an additional project.

3. I was early for the meeting, so I _____ by replying to emails.

4. I _____ when I leave work early. The traffic is lighter and I get home more quickly.

5. It is hard to balance work and family, but I try to _____ with my kids every day.

VOCABULARY EXTENSION   UNIT 2

The prefixes *in-* and *im-* can be added to some adjectives to give them the opposite meaning. For example, *independent* means "not dependent (on someone or something)."

A Circle the best word to complete each sentence.

1. I saw an online article with some **correct / incorrect** information—it said the largest ocean is the Atlantic when, in fact, it is the Pacific.

2. We cannot finish the report yet because our data is **complete / incomplete**. We are still waiting for more results.

3. It can be really **expensive / inexpensive** for schools to provide every student with a laptop or tablet computer. I don't think many schools can afford it.

4. The exam was only 50 minutes long. No one could finish it—it is **possible / impossible** to answer all those questions in such a short period of time.

5. He got 100 percent on his test—that's a(n) **perfect / imperfect** score!

WORD PARTNERS verb + *up*

Some collocations are in the verb + adverb form. Below are definitions of common collocations with the adverb *up*.

grow up: to become older

give up: to stop doing something halfway

take up: to start a new hobby, class, job, etc.

make (something) up: to invent a story that's not true

look (something) up: to search for information in a reference book or online

B Complete each sentence with the correct form of the collocations from the box above.

1. I _____ in a small village, but moved to the city when I was 18.

2. I didn't know the meaning of the word, so I _____ it _____ in a dictionary.

3. I couldn't remember a good children's story, so I _____ one _____ using my imagination.

4. I always loved taking photos, so I decided to _____ a class on photography.

5. Playing the drums was very difficult for me, but I practiced a lot and didn't _____.

VOCABULARY EXTENSION   UNIT 3

Some collocations are in the verb + noun form. Below are definitions of common collocations with the noun *control*.

take control: to have power or authority over something

lose control: not have power or authority over something

give (someone) control: to allow someone else to have power or authority

get (something) under control: to manage a situation better

get out of control: not manage a situation properly

A Circle the correct phrase to complete each sentence.

1. After my father retired, I became president and **took control** / **lost control** of the family business.

2. Drivers were unhappy because gas prices **got under control** / **got out of control**. Prices rose over 50 percent in just one month.

3. Online testing software **gives teachers control** / **gets teachers under control** over when and where they can give their students tests.

4. My laptop stopped working in the middle of my presentation. I was surprised but managed to **get out of control** / **get things under control**.

5. The man **gave control** / **lost control** of his car and crashed into a tree. The car was damaged but he was okay.

WORD PARTNERS *natural* + noun

Some collocations are in the adjective + noun form. Below are definitions of common collocations with the adjective *natural*.

natural reaction: normal human behavior

natural food: food that has no artificial ingredients added

natural disaster: an extreme event such as an earthquake or a hurricane

natural resources: useful raw materials such as minerals, trees, oil, and water

natural history: the study of animals, plants, and natural objects

B Complete each sentence with the words below.

> disasters   foods   history   reaction   resources

1. Hurricane Katrina was one of the worst natural _____ to hit the United States.

2. Many natural _____ museums have dinosaur fossils.

3. It is a natural _____ to laugh when someone tickles you.

4. Conservationists think we should protect and preserve our natural _____ for future generations.

5. Supermarkets have seen increasing demand for natural _____ in recent years.

VOCABULARY EXTENSION UNIT 4

A Complete the paragraph with the words below.

> recycled   removing   rethink   reuse

We produce over 1.3 billion tons of trash every year. This is too much. How can we reduce the amount of trash we throw away? One way is to ¹ _____ our idea of what trash actually is. Instead of throwing out an item, we could ² _____ it for a different purpose. For example, an empty glass bottle could be used as a vase for flowers. Additionally, we should sort our trash and separate items made of plastic, glass, and paper. Items of these materials can often be ³ _____ into a different product. Thankfully, many people are now ⁴ _____ items from their trash that can be recycled.

B Match each word to its antonym. Use a dictionary to help you.

_____ 1. create   a. clean

_____ 2. give   b. increase

_____ 3. reduce   c. solution

_____ 4. dirty   d. receive

_____ 5. problem   e. destroy

_____ 6. throw away   f. keep

C Choose three of the words in exercise B and write a sentence using each one.

_____

_____

_____

VOCABULARY EXTENSION   UNIT 5

Some words can be both nouns and verbs. Some examples are *offer*, *pick*, and *taste*. If a word follows an adjective, it is more likely to be a noun.

*I love the sweet **taste** of apples. They **taste** so fresh.*
           NOUN   VERB

A Read the sentences below. Label each underlined word as N for *noun* or V for *verb*.

1. A good meal <u>starts</u> with a great recipe.

2. It is okay to use frozen vegetables, but fresh <u>produce</u> is better.

3. In the summertime, it's fun to <u>cook</u> chicken or steaks on an outdoor <u>grill</u>.

4. He usually <u>times</u> his meals perfectly. Everything is ready before guests arrive.

5. This fresh bread <u>tastes</u> great, and the <u>smell</u> is amazing.

6. Everyone thought the dessert was a nice <u>treat</u>.

	ADJECTIVE	ADVERB
Many adverbs are formed by adding *-ly* to the end of adjectives. For adjectives ending in *-le*, replace the final *-e* with *-y*. For adjectives ending in *-y*, remove the final *-y* and add *-ily*.	*quick*	*quickly*
	predictable	*predictably*
	easy	*easily*

B Circle the correct words to complete the paragraph below.

Gingered Pineapple Ice Cream Sundae with Toasted Coconut

This wonderful treat was one of the most popular recipes in Sasha Martin's family. It is [1] **popular / popularly** in Sub-Saharan Africa and can be made [2] **easy / easily** with a few [3] **simple / simply** ingredients.

First, [4] **careful / carefully** cut a pineapple into small pieces and cook with ginger and brown sugar for 10 minutes. Then, pour the hot pineapple sauce over two [5] **large / largely** spoons of vanilla ice cream. [6] **Quick / Quickly** add some coconut flakes on top. The sundae is ready to eat!

VOCABULARY EXTENSION   UNIT 6

WORD LINK -able

Some adjectives end in the suffix -able which means "able to." For example, sociable means "able to be social."

A Circle the correct form of the word to complete each sentence.

1. Social robots are **suit** / **suitable** to use even with very young children.

2. Experts **predict** / **predictable** that smart technology will be a big part of our lives in the future.

3. These days, some phones allow people to use their voice to **control** / **controllable** functions like doing a search online or writing an email.

4. I would like a robot that is **adapt** / **adaptable** to different tasks, such as cooking, cleaning, and taking care of a pet.

5. Not everyone may feel **comfort** / **comfortable** with using new forms of technology.

WORD FORMS Changing Verbs into Nouns

Adding -ment to some verbs can change them into nouns. A noun with the suffix -ment means "the action or result" of doing the verb.	VERB	NOUN
	move	movement
	equip	equipment

B Complete each sentence with the correct noun form of the words below.

> assign   equip   govern   measure   state

1. People need special _____ to help them breathe on Mars.

2. In 2010, the U.S. _____ gave NASA permission to develop manned missions to Mars.

3. In a recent _____, NASA said they plan to put humans on Mars by 2040.

4. Today, scientists are taking _____ on Mars's surface to better understand the planet's environment.

5. NASA announces their crew _____ on its website by posting a list of people who are going to be working at the International Space Station.

VOCABULARY EXTENSION   UNIT 7

We use words like *deep, high, long,* and *wide* to talk about the size of an object. These words have an adjective and a noun form.

ADJECTIVE	NOUN
deep	*depth*
high	*height*
long	*length*
wide	*width*

A Complete each sentence with a measurement word from the box above.

1. The _____ of a day on Earth is about 24 hours.

2. Some volcanoes are above ground, but some are _____ below the ocean surface.

3. The mountain Mauna Kea in the Pacific Ocean is over 10,000 meters _____. But only a third of it is visible above the ocean.

4. Growing to a _____ of over a hundred meters, the Californian redwoods are the tallest trees in the world.

5. The original Panama Canal was just over 30 meters _____, but many ships were too big to fit through it. To solve this problem, engineers increased the _____ of the Canal.

Some collocations are in the verb + adverb/preposition form. Below are definitions of common collocations with the verb *run*.

run into: to meet someone by chance

run out (of): to have no supplies left

run after: to follow or chase something or someone

run away (from): to leave somewhere because you are unhappy there

run up: to make something (e.g., a bill, debt, or score) become bigger

B Match the sentence parts in the columns to complete each sentence.

_____ 1. I ran into

_____ 2. I ran after

_____ 3. I ran up

_____ 4. I ran out of

_____ 5. Instead of running away from

a. your problems, talk to someone about them.

b. a huge bill at the hotel.

c. my childhood friend this morning.

d. paint before I had finished the project.

e. the bus and got on it just in time.

VOCABULARY EXTENSION   UNIT 8

A   Circle the best word to complete each sentence.

1. Some people **disbelieve** / **dislike** rock music. They think it's too loud.

2. My friends have strong **disagreements** / **disadvantages** about which band is the best.

3. The sound of classical music and pop music is **dissimilar** / **disinterested** in many ways.

4. Some parents think it's a **disagreement** / **disadvantage** for children not to learn a musical instrument.

5. Although Stevie Wonder couldn't see, he didn't let his **disability** / **distrust** stop him from learning several musical instruments and becoming a famous artist.

B   Complete each sentence with the correct noun form of the adjectives below.

> adaptable   electric   popular   possible   responsible

1. The _____ of rap music continues to increase among young people.

2. Some musicians feel they have a(n) _____ to use their influence and create positive change.

3. Some modern musical instruments, like keyboards, require _____ to produce sound.

4. People's music preferences can change quickly, so _____ is an important quality in order for musicians to succeed.

5. In the future, there is a(n) _____ that people will only listen to music through online music streaming services.

VOCABULARY EXTENSION   UNIT 9

Nouns that end with the suffixes *-er* and *-or* often refer to "a person or thing that does something." For example, a *trainer* is someone who trains people or animals.

A Complete each sentence with the correct noun form of the words below. Add *a* or *an*.

> compose   farm   instruct   own   visit

1. Someone who has a pet is _____.

2. Someone who grows crops is _____.

3. Someone who writes music is called _____.

4. Someone who teaches in a college is _____.

5. Someone who goes to a tourist attraction is _____.

WORD FORMS Homonyms

Homonyms are words that are spelled and pronounced in the same way but have different meanings. For example, a *bat* is a thick wooden stick used in some sports. A *bat* is also a small flying mammal.

B Match each word (1–5) with the two best definitions.

a. just; equal

b. a living organism

c. light-haired or light-skinned

d. strength of mind

e. a factory

f. a subject area

g. a clue; a piece of information

h. an important role in a play or movie

i. a type of legal document

j. an area of land

1. fair   _____, _____

2. field   _____, _____

3. lead   _____, _____

4. plant   _____, _____

5. will   _____, _____

VOCABULARY EXTENSION   UNIT 10

WORD LINK *vis*

Words containing *vis* and *vid* usually have meanings that are related to "seeing."
Some examples are *visit* and *video*.

A   Complete each sentence with the words below. Use a dictionary to help you.

> invisible   revised   videos   visitors   visuals

1. After receiving feedback from her instructor, she ＿＿＿＿＿ her essay.

2. Websites like YouTube allow people to share their ＿＿＿＿＿ easily.

3. Hundreds of ＿＿＿＿＿ came to the opening of the new photography exhibition.

4. She uses a special camera to photograph tiny creatures that are almost ＿＿＿＿＿ to the human eye.

5. Some people enjoy reading graphic novels and comics because they contain a lot of colorful ＿＿＿＿＿.

WORD FORMS   Changing Verbs into Adjectives

Some adjectives are formed by adding *-ed* and *-ing* to verbs. Adjectives ending in *-ed*
describe how someone feels. Adjectives ending in *-ing* describe the characteristic of
someone or something.

The leopard seal looked frightening. The photographer was frightened.

B   Circle the correct adjectives to complete the paragraph.

My favorite photo is of my family having dinner. It is an [1] **interested / interesting** picture—everyone in the

photo has a different expression. My husband is [2] **surprised / surprising** because our cat has just jumped

on the table. My son looks [3] **disappointed / disappointing** because there is no more dessert. My mother is

[4] **concerned / concerning** about all the mess. We had a lot of cleaning up to do afterward, but the huge

dinner was [5] **satisfied / satisfying**.

Independent Student Handbook

TIPS FOR READING FLUENTLY

Reading slowly, one word at a time, makes it difficult to get an overall sense of the meaning of a text. As a result, reading becomes more challenging and less interesting. In general, it is a good idea to first skim a text for the gist, and then read it again more closely so that you can focus on the most relevant details. Use these strategies to improve your reading speed:

- Read groups of words rather than individual words.
- Keep your eyes moving forward. Read through to the end of each sentence or paragraph instead of going back to reread words or phrases.
- Skip functional words (articles, prepositions, etc.) and focus on words and phrases carrying meaning—the content words.
- Use clues in the text—such as **bold** words and words in *italics*—to help you know which parts might be important and worth focusing on.
- Use section headings, as well as the first and last lines of paragraphs, to help you understand how the text is organized.
- Use context clues, affixes and parts of speech—instead of a dictionary—to guess the meaning of unfamiliar words and phrases.

TIPS FOR READING CRITICALLY

As you read, ask yourself questions about what the writer is saying, and how and why the writer is presenting the information at hand.

Important critical thinking skills for academic reading and writing:

- **Analyzing:** Examining a text in close detail in order to identify key points, similarities, and differences.
- **Applying:** Deciding how ideas or information might be relevant in a different context, e.g., applying possible solutions to problems.
- **Evaluating:** Using evidence to decide how relevant, important, or useful something is. This often involves looking at reasons for and against something.
- **Inferring:** "Reading between the lines;" in other words, identifying what a writer is saying indirectly, or implicitly, rather than directly, or explicitly.
- **Synthesizing:** Gathering appropriate information and ideas from more than one source and making a judgment, summary, or conclusion based on the evidence.
- **Reflecting:** Relating ideas and information in a text to your own personal experience and viewpoints.

TIPS FOR NOTE-TAKING

Taking notes will help you better understand the overall meaning and organization of a text. Note-taking also helps you to record the most important information for future uses—such as when you have a writing assignment. Use these techniques to make your note-taking more effective.

- As you read, underline or highlight important information such as dates, names, places, and other facts.
- Take notes in the margin. Note the main idea and supporting details next to each paragraph. Also note your own ideas or questions about the paragraph.
- On a separate piece of paper, write notes about the key points of the text in your own words. Include short headings, key words, page numbers, and quotations.
- Keep your notes brief by using these abbreviations and symbols. For an example of how they are used, see page 148.

approx.	approximately
e.g./ex.	example
i.e.	that is / in other words
p. (pp.)	page (pages)
re:	regarding, concerning
yr(s)	year(s)
➔	leads to / causes
& or +	and
b/c	because
w/	with

TIPS FOR LEARNING VOCABULARY

You often need to use a word or phrase several times before it enters your long-term memory. Here are some strategies for successfully learning vocabulary:

- Use flash cards to test your knowledge of new vocabulary. Write the words you want to learn on one side of an index card. Write the definition and/or an example sentence that uses the word on the other side.

- Use a vocabulary journal to note down a new word or phrase. Write a short definition of the word in English and the sentence where you found it. Write another sentence of your own that uses the word. Include any common collocations (see *Word Partners* in the Vocabulary Extensions).

- Make word webs or word maps. See below for an example.

- Use memory aids to remember a word or phrase. For example, if you want to learn the idiom *keep an eye on someone*, which means to "watch someone carefully," you might picture yourself putting your eyeball on someone's shoulder so that you can watch the person carefully. The stranger the picture is, the more likely you will remember it!

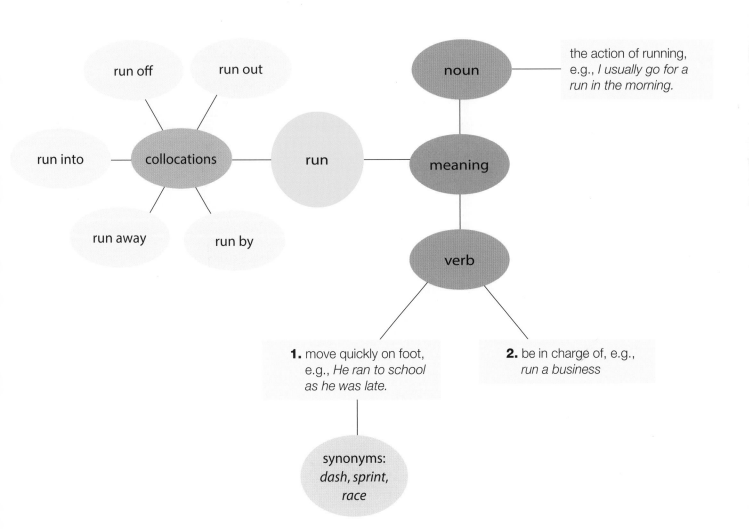

TIPS FOR ACADEMIC WRITING

There are many types of academic writing (descriptive, argumentative/persuasive, narrative, etc.), but most types share similar characteristics. Generally, in academic writing you should:

- write in full sentences.
- use formal English. (Avoid slang or conversational expressions such as *kind of*.)
- be clear and coherent—keep to your main point; avoid technical words that the reader may not know.
- use signal words or phrases and conjunctions to connect your ideas. (See examples below.)
- have a clear point (main idea) for each paragraph.
- use a neutral point of view—avoid overuse of personal pronouns (*I*, *we*, *you*) and subjective language such as *nice* or *terrible*.
- use facts, examples, and expert opinions to support your argument.
- avoid using abbreviations or language used in texting. (Use *that is* rather than *i.e.*, and *in my opinion*, not *IMO*.)
- avoid using contractions. (Use *is not* rather than *isn't*.)
- avoid starting sentences with *or*, *and*, or *but*.

Signal Phrases

Use signal words and phrases to connect ideas and to make your writing more academic.

Giving supporting details and examples	Describing a process
One / An example of this is … For example, … / For instance, …	First (of all), … Then / Next / After that, … As soon as … / When … Finally, …
Giving reasons	**Presenting contrasting ideas**
This is because (of) … One reason (for this) is …	However, … In contrast, …
Describing cause and effect	**Giving an opinion**
Therefore, … As a result, … Because of this, …	In my opinion, … I think / feel that … I believe (that) …

TIPS FOR EDITING

Capitalization

Remember to capitalize:

- the first letter of the word at the beginning of every sentence.

- proper names such as names of people, geographical names, company names, and names of organizations.

- days, months, and holidays.

- the word *I*.

- the first letter of a title such as the title of a movie or a book.

- the words in titles that have meaning (content words). Don't capitalize *a, an, the, and*, or prepositions such as *to, for, of, from, at, in*, and *on*, unless they are the first word of a title (e.g., *The First Grader*).

Punctuation

- Use a period (.) at the end of any sentence that is not a question.

- Exclamation marks (!), which indicate strong feelings such as surprise or joy, are generally not used in academic writing.

- Use commas (,) to separate a list of three or more things. (*She speaks German, English, and Spanish*.)

- Use a comma after an introductory word or phrase. (*In contrast, apes can live almost 60 years*.)

- Use a comma before a combining word—*and, but, so, or*—that joins two sentences. (*People will visit Mars, and they will build habitation modules*.)

- Use an apostrophe (') for showing possession. (*Mars's polar regions will begin to melt, releasing more carbon dioxide trapped inside the ice*.)

- Use quotation marks (" ") to indicate the exact words used by someone else. (*"Sometimes we see ourselves as so small," says Irma, a cook at Gramacho*.)

Other Proofreading Tips

- Print out your draft and read it out loud.

- Use a colored pen to make corrections on your draft so you can see them easily when you write your next draft.

- Have someone else read your draft and give you comments or ask you questions.

- Don't depend on a computer's spell-check. When the spell-check suggests a correction, make sure you agree with it before you accept the change.

- Check the spelling and accuracy of proper nouns, numbers, and dates.

- Keep a list of spelling and grammar mistakes that you commonly make so that you can be aware of them as you edit your draft.

- Check for frequently confused words:

  - *there, their*, and *they're*
  - *its* and *it's*
  - *your* and *you're*
  - *to, too*, and *two*
  - *whose* and *who's*
  - *where, wear, we're*, and *were*

EDITING CHECKLIST

Use the checklist to find errors in the second draft of your writing task for each unit.

	Unit				
	1	2	3	4	5
1. Is the first word of every sentence capitalized?					
2. Does every sentence end with the correct punctuation?					
3. Do your subjects and verbs agree?					
4. Are commas used in the right places?					
5. Do all possessive nouns have an apostrophe?					
6. Are all proper nouns capitalized?					
7. Is the spelling of places, people, and other proper nouns correct?					
8. Did you check for frequently confused words (see examples on page 217)?					

	Unit				
	6	7	8	9	10
1. Is the first word of every sentence capitalized?					
2. Does every sentence end with the correct punctuation?					
3. Do your subjects and verbs agree?					
4. Are commas used in the right places?					
5. Do all possessive nouns have an apostrophe?					
6. Are all proper nouns capitalized?					
7. Is the spelling of places, people, and other proper nouns correct?					
8. Did you check for frequently confused words (see examples on page 217)?					

GRAMMAR REFERENCE

UNIT 1
Language for Writing: Simple Present of *Be* and Other Verbs

Affirmative and Negative Statements with *Be*

Affirmative Statements			Negative Statements		
Subject	**Am/Are/Is**		**Subject**	**Am/Are/Is**	
I	**am**		I	**am not**	
You We They	**are**	happy. sad. here. at work.	You We They	**are not**	happy. sad. here. at work.
He She It	**is**		He She It	**is not**	

Affirmative and Negative Statements: Other Verbs

Affirmative Statements		Negative Statements		
Subject	**Verb**	**Subject**	**Do/Does Not**	**Verb (Base Form)**
I You We They	**work** in an office.	I You We They	**do not** **don't**	**work** in a laboratory.
He She It	**works** in an office.	He She It	**does not** **doesn't**	

UNIT 3
Language for Writing: Connecting Ideas

The words and phrases below help connect ideas between sentences.

Notes	Examples
Use *in addition, furthermore*, and *also* to give additional information about an idea.	Advertisers know that consumers like watching their favorite celebrities. **Furthermore**, consumers are willing to buy products featuring celebrities.
Add a comma after the transition word or phrase that comes at the beginning of a sentence.	**In addition**, celebrities can help reach a larger number of people.
Some transition words or phrases can be put before the main verb. Add commas before and after the transition word or phrase.	Celebrities can, **in addition**, help reach a larger number of people.
Also does not usually need commas when used.	Celebrities can **also** help reach a larger number of people.

UNIT 5
Language for Writing: Giving Reasons

Use the transition word *because* to show a reason.

Notes	Examples
Because is a conjunction. It connects ideas between sentences. It shows a reason.	REASON Adam Roberts started a food blog **because he needed a break**.
Because introduces a dependent clause. A dependent clause must have a subject and a verb.	DEPENDENT CLAUSE Roberts started a food blog because **he needed** a break. SUBJECT VERB
The dependent clause with *because* can start a sentence. Add a comma to separate the clauses.	**Because** he needed a break from school, Roberts started a food blog.

Use *in order* to show a reason.

Notes	Examples
Use *in order* with an infinitive to show a reason.	Some people start blogs **in order** <u>to tell their friends about their daily lives</u>. REASON
The infinitive can be used without *in order*.	Some people start blogs **to tell** their friends about their daily lives.

UNIT 6
Language for Writing: Coordinating Conjunctions

And, but, and *so* are coordinating conjunctions. They can connect single words, phrases, or clauses.

Notes	Example
Use *and* to connect or add information.	Students are are studying Mars **and** Venus.
	People will visit Mars **and** build habitation modules.
	People will visit Mars, **and** they will build habitation modules.
Use *but* to show contrast.	Mars is cold **but** habitable.
	People have traveled to the moon **but** not to Mars.
	People have traveled to the moon, **but** they haven't traveled to Mars.
Use *so* to show result.	It is very cold on Mars, **so** we will need to warm it up.
Remove repeated subjects in the second clause.	Mars is very cold **and** (M̶a̶r̶s̶) has no oxygen.
Remove repeated verbs and auxiliary verbs in the second clause.	People will live **and** (w̶i̶l̶l̶) work on Mars.

UNIT 8
Language for Writing: Using Time Expressions

Use prepositions of time to show what happened in a person's life.

Notes	Examples
Use *in* for months, years, and specific periods of time.	Yo-Yo Ma was born in Paris **in** 1955.
Use *on* for specific dates.	**On** July 5, 1986, Ma performed a concert in New York City.
Use *before* for an earlier time.	Ma lived in Paris **before** 1962.
Use *after* for a later time.	**After** 1962, Ma moved to New York.
Use *during* to indicate a period of time an event or events happened for.	**During** the concert, Ma played the cello.

Time clauses help show the order of events in someone's life. A time clause includes time words such as *after*, *before*, and *when*.

Notes	Examples
Use a comma after the time clause.	TIME CLAUSE **After** Ma moved to New York, he attended the Julliard School of Music.
A time clause can come at the end of a sentence. No comma is needed.	Ma attended the Julliard School of Music **after** he moved to New York.
Use *after* to show the first event. Use *before* to show the next event.	**After** Ma moved to New York, he attended the Julliard School of Music. **Before** Ma attended the Julliard School of Music, he moved to New York. (First he moved to New York, then he attended the Julliard School of Music.)
Use *when* to show the time an event first started.	He started playing the cello **when he was 4 years old**. **When he was 4 years old**, he learned to play the cello.

UNIT 9
Language for Writing: Making Comparisons

Use the following words and phrases to show similarities within sentences. Notice that we use a comma after the phrase with *like*.

Both … and	**Both** gorillas **and** humans are primates.
Like	**Like** humans, chimpanzees show their young how to use tools.
Neither … nor	**Neither** Labradors nor Australian terriers are difficult dogs to train.

Use *similarly* and *likewise* to show similarities between sentences. Notice that we use a comma after these words.

Similarly	Chimpanzees can learn sign language. **Similarly**, parrots can learn to communicate with humans.
Likewise	Cats can live in small apartments. **Likewise**, some dog breeds do well in small spaces.

Use the following words to show differences within sentences. Notice that we use a comma after phrases with *unlike* and *while*.

Unlike	**Unlike** cats, dogs are very dependent on their owners.
Whereas	Dogs will eat anything, **whereas** cats are more particular about their diet.
While	**While** dogs need to be bathed, cats can clean themselves.

Use the following words and phrases to show differences between sentences. Notice that we use a comma after each one.

However	Gorillas can weigh up to 400 pounds (181 kg). **However**, chimpanzees only weigh about 100 pounds (45 kg).
In contrast	Domesticated animals make good pets. **In contrast**, wild animals are dangerous and may attack humans.
On the other hand	I like dogs. My brother, **on the other hand**, prefers cats.

VOCABULARY INDEX

Word	Unit	CEFR Level	Word	Unit	CEFR Level
according to	10	B1	disabled	8	B1
adapt*	6	B2	disappointed	10	B1
advice	2	A2	discover	7	B1
ancient	7	B1	dish (n)	5	A2
angry	9	A2	documentary	8	B1
appearance	8	B1	during	1	A2
approach* (n)	9	B2	education	2	B1
argue	5	B1	element*	10	B2
arrive	1	A2	emotion	10	B2
artifact	7	-	encourage	8	B1
attend	2	B1	energetic*	8	B2
attitude*	3	B1	environment*	6	B1
attractive	3	A2	escape (v)	8	B1
audience	8	B1	exist	7	B1
average (adj)	6	B1	expect	9	B1
avoid	3	B1	experience (v)	7	B1
aware*	4	B2	extraordinary	1	B1
balance (v)	1	B2	extremely	7	B1
believe	2	A2	fair (adj)	9	B1
belong	10	B2	float	4	B1
bond* (n)	8	B2	fresh	5	A2
calm	10	B1	fried	5	A2
capture	10	B2	frightened	10	B1
cash	3	A2	give up	2	B1
cause (v)	4	B2	government	2	B1
ceremony	10	B1	hidden	7	B1
challenging*	7	B1	hope	5	A2
clean up	4	A1	image*	4	B2
collect	4	A2	immediately	10	A2
communicate*	1	B1	improve	8	A2
companion	9	B2	incredible	10	B1
composer	8	B2	independent	2	B1
confused	9	B1	influence (v)	3	B2
connect	1	B1	ingredient	5	B1
continue	9	B1	instead of	3	A2
control (v)	3	B1	instrument	8	A2
cooperate*	9	B2	intelligent*	6	B1
create*	4	B1	issue* (v)	8	B1
creature	7	B1	kill	4	A2
culture*	5	B1	lack (n)	6	B1
customer	3	A2	leader	2	B1
deal with	4	B1	level (n)	6	A2
decide	2	A2	limit (n)	3	B1
deep	7	A2	link* (v)	6	B2
depend on	1	B1	liquid	6	B1
develop	2	B1	located*	7	B1

Word	Unit	CEFR Level	Word	Unit	CEFR Level
massive	7	B2	respect (v)	5	B1
material	4	B1	response*	9	B2
measure (v)	1	B2	responsibility	8	B2
message (n)	3	A1	reward (n)	9	B1
motivated*	2	B2	risk (v)	7	B2
natural	3	B1	run out	7	B1
network*	6	B2	scene	10	B1
normal*	1	A2	schedule* (n)	1	B2
notice (v)	3	A2	share (v)	5	A2
offer	5	A2	similar*	2	B1
ordinary	2	B1	situation	8	B1
organization	4	B1	skill	2	B1
owner	9	B1	sociable	6	B1
painting	4	A2	solution	4	B1
percent*	3	B1	solve	2	B1
perform	8	B1	spend time	1	A2
pet (n)	9	A1	store (n)	3	B1
pick	5	B1	store (v)	6	B2
plant (n)	6	A1	strategy*	3	B2
point out	10	B2	suddenly	10	B1
popular	5	A2	suggest	6	B1
positive*	8	B1	surface (n)	7	B2
powerful	9	B1	surprise(n)	1	A2
predict*	6	B1	take care of	1	B1
preference	6	B2	taste	5	B1
prepare	5	A2	team*	1	A2
primary*	2	B2	technology*	6	B1
probably	3	A2	throw away	4	A2
produce (v)	1	B1	trainer	9	B1
product	3	B1	trap (v)	6	B2
profession	9	B1	treat (v)	8	B2
program (n)	2	A2	trust (v)	3	B1
project* (n)	1	A2	type (n)	5	A2
proud	4	B1	typical	5	B1
quality (n)	10	B1	underground	7	A2
realize	1	B1	universe	7	B1
receive	4	A2	upload	1	B1
recipe	5	B1	variety	5	A2
record (v)	2	A2	visual*	10	B2
recycle	4	B1	willing	9	B1
region*	7	B1	work out	9	B2
relationship	10	B1			
release* (v)	6	B2			
remind	10	B1			
report (v)	4	B1			
rescue (v)	8	B1			
research* (n)	9	B1			

*These words are on the Academic Word List (AWL). The AWL is a list of the 570 most frequent word families in academic texts. It does not include the most frequent 2,000 words of English.

ACKNOWLEDGMENTS

The Authors and Publisher would like to acknowledge the teachers around the world who participated in the development of the second edition of *Pathways*.

A special thanks to our Advisory Board for their valuable input during the development of this series.

ADVISORY BOARD

Mahmoud Al Hosni, Modern College of Business and Science, Oman; **Safaa Al-Salim**, Kuwait University; **Laila Al-Qadhi**, Kuwait University; **Julie Bird**, RMIT University Vietnam; **Elizabeth Bowles**, Virginia Tech Language and Culture Institute, Blacksburg, VA; **Rachel Bricker**, Arizona State University, Tempe, AZ; **James Broadbridge**, J.F. Oberlin University, Tokyo; **Marina Broeder**, Mission College, Santa Clara, CA; **Shawn Campbell**, Hangzhou High School; **Trevor Carty**, James Cook University, Singapore; **Jindarat De Vleeschauwer**, Chiang Mai University; **Wai-Si El Hassan**, Prince Mohammad Bin Fahd University, Saudi Arabia; **Jennifer Farnell**, University of Bridgeport, Bridgeport, CT; **Rasha Gazzaz**, King Abdulaziz University, Saudi Arabia; **Keith Graziadei**, Santa Monica College, Santa Monica, CA; **Janet Harclerode**, Santa Monica Community College, Santa Monica, CA; **Anna Hasper**, TeacherTrain, UAE; **Phoebe Kamel Yacob Hindi**, Abu Dhabi Vocational Education and Training Institute, UAE; **Kuei-ping Hsu**, National Tsing Hua University; **Greg Jewell**, Drexel University, Philadelphia, PA; **Adisra Katib**, Chulalongkorn University Language Institute, Bangkok; **Wayne Kennedy**, LaGuardia Community College, Long Island City, NY; **Beth Koo**, Central Piedmont Community College, Charlotte, NC; **Denise Kray**, Bridge School, Denver, CO; **Chantal Kruger**, ILA Vietnam; **William P. Kyzner**, Fuyang AP Center; **Becky Lawrence**, Massachusetts International Academy, Marlborough, MA; **Deborah McGraw**, Syracuse University, NY; **Mary Moore**, University of Puerto Rico; **Raymond Purdy**, ELS Language Centers, Princeton, NJ; **Anouchka Rachelson**, Miami Dade College, Miami, FL; **Fathimah Razman**, Universiti Utara Malaysia; **Phil Rice**, University of Delaware ELI, Newark, DE; **Scott Rousseau**, American University of Sharjah, UAE; **Verna Santos-Nafrada**, King Saud University, Saudi Arabia; **Eugene Sidwell**, American Intercon Institute, Phnom Penh; **Gemma Thorp**, Monash University English Language Centre, Australia; **Matt Thurston**, University of Central Lancashire, UK; **Christine Tierney**, Houston Community College, Houston, TX; **Jet Robredillo Tonogbanua**, FPT University, Hanoi.

GLOBAL REVIEWERS
ASIA

Antonia Cavcic, Asia University, Tokyo; **Soyhan Egitim**, Tokyo University of Science; **Caroline Handley**, Asia University, Tokyo; **Patrizia Hayashi**, Meikai University, Urayasu; **Greg Holloway**, University of Kitakyushu; **Anne C. Ihata**, Musashino University, Tokyo; **Kathryn Mabe**, Asia University, Tokyo; **Frederick Navarro Bacala**, Yokohama City University; **Tyson Rode**, Meikai University, Urayasu; **Scott Shelton-Strong**, Asia University, Tokyo; **Brooks Slaybaugh**, Yokohama City University; **Susanto Sugiharto**, Sutomo Senior High School, Medan; **Andrew Zitzmann**, University of Kitakyushu.

LATIN AMERICA AND THE CARIBBEAN

Raul Bilini, ProLingua, Dominican Republic; **Alejandro Garcia**, Collegio Marcelina, Mexico; **Humberto Guevara**, Tec de Monterrey, Campus Monterrey, Mexico; **Romina Olga Planas**, Centro Cultural Paraguayo Americano, Paraguay; **Carlos Rico-Troncoso**, Pontificia Universidad Javeriana, Colombia; **Ialê Schetty**, Enjoy English, Brazil; **Aline Simoes**, Way To Go Private English, Brazil; **Paulo Cezar Lira Torres**, APenglish, Brazil; **Rosa Enilda Vasquez**, Swisher Dominicana, Dominican Republic; **Terry Whitty**, LDN Language School, Brazil.

MIDDLE EAST AND NORTH AFRICA

Susan Daniels, Kuwait University, Kuwait; **Mahmoud Mohammadi Khomeini**, Sokhane Ashna Language School, Iran; **Müge Lenbet**, Koç University, Turkey; **Robert Anthony Lowman**, Prince Mohammad bin Fahd University, Saudi Arabia; **Simon Mackay**, Prince Mohammad bin Fahd University, Saudi Arabia.

USA AND CANADA

Frank Abbot, Houston Community College, Houston, TX; **Hossein Aksari**, Bilingual Education Institute and Houston Community College, Houston, TX; **Sudie Allen-Henn**, North Seattle College, Seattle, WA; **Sharon Allie**, Santa Monica Community College, Santa Monica, CA; **Jerry Archer**, Oregon State University, Corvallis, OR; **Nicole Ashton**, Central Piedmont Community College, Charlotte, NC; **Barbara Barrett**, University of Miami, Coral Gables, FL; **Maria Bazan-Myrick**, Houston Community College, Houston, TX; **Rebecca Beal**, Colleges of Marin, Kentfield, CA; **Marlene Beck**, Eastern Michigan University, Ypsilanti, MI; **Michelle Bell**, University of Southern California, Los Angeles, CA; **Linda Bolet**, Houston Community College, Houston, TX; **Jenna Bollinger**, Eastern Michigan University, Ypsilanti, MI; **Monica Boney**, Houston Community College, Houston, TX; **Nanette Bouvier**, Rutgers University – Newark, Newark, NJ; **Nancy Boyer**, Golden West College, Huntington Beach, CA; **Lia Brenneman**, University of Florida English Language Institute, Gainesville, FL; **Colleen Brice**, Grand Valley State University, Allendale, MI; **Kristen Brown**, Massachusetts International Academy, Marlborough, MA; **Philip Brown**, Houston Community College, Houston, TX; **Dongmei Cao**, San Jose City College, San Jose, CA; **Molly Cheney**, University of Washington, Seattle, WA; **Emily Clark**, The University of Kansas, Lawrence, KS; **Luke Coffelt**, International English Center, Boulder, CO; **William C Cole-French**, MCPHS University;

Boston, MA; **Charles Colson**, English Language Institute at Sam Houston State University, Huntsville, TX; **Lucy Condon**, Bilingual Education Institute, Houston, TX; **Janice Crouch**, Internexus Indiana, Indianapolis, IN; **Charlene Dandrow**, Virginia Tech Language and Culture Institute, Blacksburg, VA; **Loretta Davis**, Coastline Community College, Westminster, CA; **Marta Dmytrenko-Ahrabian**, Wayne State University, Detroit, MI; **Bonnie Duhart**, Houston Community College, Houston, TX; **Karen Eichhorn**, International English Center, Boulder, CO; **Tracey Ellis**, Santa Monica Community College, Santa Monica, CA; **Jennifer Evans**, University of Washington, Seattle, WA; **Marla Ewart**, Bilingual Education Institute, Houston, TX; **Rhoda Fagerland**, St. Cloud State University, St. Cloud, MN; **Kelly Montijo Fink**, Kirkwood Community College, Cedar Rapids, IA; **Celeste Flowers**, University of Central Arkansas, Conway, AR; **Kurtis Foster**, Missouri State University, Springfield, MO; **Rachel Garcia**, Bilingual Education Institute, Houston, TX; **Thomas Germain**, University of Colorado Boulder, Boulder, CO; **Claire Gimble**, Virginia International University, Fairfax, VA; **Marilyn Glazer-Weisner**, Middlesex Community College, Lowell, MA; **Amber Goodall**, South Piedmont Community College, Charlotte, NC; **Katya Goussakova**, Seminole State College of Florida, Sanford, FL; **Jane Granado**, Texas State University, San Marcos, TX; **Therea Hampton**, Mercer County Community College, West Windsor Township, NJ; **Jane Hanson**, University of Nebraska – Lincoln, Lincoln, NE; **Lauren Heather**, University of Texas at San Antonio, San Antonio, TX; **Jannette Hermina**, Saginaw Valley State University, Saginaw, MI; **Gail Hernandez**, College of Staten Island, Staten Island, NY; **Beverly Hobbs**, Clark University, Worcester, MA; **Kristin Homuth**, Language Center International, Southfield, MI; **Tim Hooker**, Campbellsville University, Campbellsville, KY; **Raylene Houck**, Idaho State University, Pocatello, ID; **Karen L. Howling**, University of Bridgeport, Bridgeport, CT; **Sharon Jaffe**, Santa Monica Community College, Santa Monica, CA; **Andrea Kahn**, Santa Monica Community College, Santa Monica, CA; **Eden Bradshaw Kaiser**, Massachusetts International Academy, Marlborough, MA; **Mandy Kama**, Georgetown University, Washington, D.C.; **Andrea Kaminski**, University of Michigan – Dearborn, Dearborn, MI; **Eileen Kramer**, Boston University CELOP, Brookline, MA; **Rachel Lachance**, University of New Hampshire, Durham, NH; **Janet Langon**, Glendale Community College, Glendale, CA; **Frances Le Grand**, University of Houston, Houston, TX; **Esther Lee**, California State University, Fullerton, CA; **Helen S. Mays Lefal**, American Learning Institute, Dallas, TX; **Oranit Limmaneeprasert**, American River College, Sacramento, CA; **Dhammika Liyanage**, Bilingual Education Institute, Houston, TX; **Emily Lodmer**, Santa Monica Community College, Santa Monica Community College, CA; **Ari Lopez**, American Learning Institute Dallas, TX; **Nichole Lukas**, University of Dayton, Dayton, OH; **Undarmaa Maamuujav**, California State University, Los Angeles, CA; **Diane Mahin**, University of Miami, Coral Gables, FL; **Melanie Majeski**, Naugatuck Valley Community College, Waterbury, CT; **Judy Marasco**, Santa Monica Community College, Santa Monica, CA; **Murray McMahan**, University of Alberta, Alberta; **Deirdre McMurtry**, University of Nebraska Omaha, Omaha, NE; **Suzanne Meyer**, University of Pittsburgh, Pittsburgh, PA; **Cynthia Miller**, Richland College, Dallas, TX; **Sara Miller**, Houston Community College, Houston, TX; **Gwendolyn Miraglia**, Houston Community College, Houston, TX; **Katie Mitchell**, International English Center, Boulder, CO; **Ruth Williams Moore**, University of Colorado Boulder, Boulder, CO; **Kathy Najafi**, Houston Community College, Houston, TX; **Sandra Navarro**, Glendale Community College, Glendale, CA; **Stephanie Ngom**, Boston University, Boston MA; **Barbara Niemczyk**, University of Bridgeport, Bridgeport, CT; **Melody Nightingale**, Santa Monica Community College, Santa Monica, CA; **Alissa Olgun**, California Language Academy, Los Angeles, CA; **Kimberly Oliver**, Austin Community College, Austin, TX; **Steven Olson**, International English Center, Boulder, CO; **Fernanda Ortiz**, University of Arizona, Tucson, AZ; **Joel Ozretich**, University of Washington, Seattle, WA; **Erin Pak**, Schoolcraft College, Livonia, MI; **Geri Pappas**, University of Michigan – Dearborn, Dearborn, MI; **Eleanor Paterson**, Erie Community College, Buffalo, NY; **Sumeeta Patnaik**, Marshall University, Huntington, WV; **Mary Peacock**, Richland College, Dallas, TX; **Kathryn Porter**, University of Houston, Houston, TX; **Eileen Prince**, Prince Language Associates, Newton Highlands, MA; **Marina Ramirez**, Houston Community College, Houston, TX; **Laura Ramm**, Michigan State University, East Lansing, MI; **Chi Rehg**, University of South Florida, Tampa, FL; **Cyndy Reimer**, Douglas College, New Westminister, BC, Canada; **Sydney Rice**, Imperial Valley College, Imperial, CA; **Lynnette Robson**, Mercer University, Macon, GA; **Helen E. Roland**, Miami Dade College, Miami, FL; **Maria Paula Carreira Rolim**, Southeast Missouri State University, Cape Girardeau, MO; **Jill Rolston-Yates**, Texas State University, San Marcos, TX; **David Ross**, Houston Community College, Houston, TX; **Rachel Scheiner**, Seattle Central College, Seattle, WA; **John Schmidt**, Texas Intensive English Program, Austin, TX; **Mariah Schueman**, University of Miami, Coral Gables, FL; **Erika Shadburne**, Austin Community College, Austin, TX; **Mahdi Shamsi**, Houston Community College, Houston, TX; **Osha Sky**, Highline College, Des Moines, WA; **William Slade**, University of Texas, Austin, TX; **Takako Smith**, University of Nebraska – Lincoln, Lincoln, NE; **Barbara Smith-Palinkas**, Hillsborough Community College, Tampa, FL; **Paula Snyder**, University of Missouri, Columbia, MO; **Mary; Evelyn Sorrell**, Bilingual Education Institute, Houston TX; **Kristen Stauffer**, International English Center, Boulder, CO; **Christina Stefanik**, The Language Company, Toledo, OH; **Cory Stewart**, University of Houston, Houston, TX; **Laurie Stusser-McNeill**, Highline College, Des Moines, WA; **Tom Sugawara**, University of Washington, Seattle, WA; **Sara Sulko**, University of Missouri, Columbia, MO; **Mark Sullivan**, University of Colorado Boulder, Boulder, CO; **Olivia Szabo**, Boston University, Boston, MA; **Amber Tallent**, University of Nebraska Omaha, Omaha, NE; **Amy Tate**, Rice University, Houston, USA; **Aya C. Tiacoh**, Bilingual Education Institute, Houston, TX; **Troy Tucker**, Florida SouthWestern State College, Fort Myers, FL; **Anne Tyoan**, Savannah College of Art and Design, Savannah, GA; **Michael Vallee**, International English Center, Boulder, CO; **Andrea Vasquez**, University of Southern Maine, Portland, ME; **Jose Vasquez**, University of Texas Rio Grande Valley, Edinburg, TX; **Maureen Vendeville**, Savannah Technical College, Savannah, GA; **Melissa Vervinck**, Oakland University, Rochester, MI; **Adriana Villarreal**, Universided Nacional Autonoma de Mexico, San Antonio, TX; **Summer Webb**, International English Center, Boulder, CO; **Mercedes Wilson-Everett**, Houston Community College, Houston, TX; **Lora Yasen**, Tokyo International University of America, Salem, OR; **Dennis Yommer**, Youngstown State University, Youngstown, OH; **Melojeane (Jolene) Zawilinski**, University of Michigan – Flint, Flint, MI.

CREDITS

Photos

Cover, **iii** Babak Tafreshi/National Geographic Creative, **iv** (from top to bottom) © Martin Roemers/Panos, © Austin Turner, pius99/Getty Images, © Gregg Segal, © Soma Chakraborty Debnath, **vi** (from top to bottom) Yuriko Nakao/Reuters, Wes C. Skiles/National Geographic Creative, Michael Wheatley/Alamy Stock Photo, Joel Sartore/National Geographic Photo Ark, Cameron Spencer/Getty Images, **1** (c) © Martin Roemers/Panos, **2–3** © Globaia, **5** © Vania da Rui, **6** Dave M. Benett/Getty Images, **9** © Courtesy of Do Remember Me, **12–13** (c) © Ricky Qi, **13** (tr) © WHOI, **13** (br) Charlotte Stanford/National Geographic Creative, **21** © Austin Turner, **25** Thomas Mukoya/Reuters, **26** Thomas Mukoya/Reuters, **28** Philip Scott Andrews/National Geographic Creative, **29** Joel van Houdt/National Geographic Creative, **32–33** (t) Keith Ladzinski/National Geographic Creative, **33** (br) keith morris news/Alamy Stock Photo, **41** pius99/Getty Images, **42–43** Gerd Ludwig/National Geographic Creative, **45** Roberto Machado Noa/Getty Images, **46** Brooks Kraft/Getty Images, **47** Cengage Learning, **49** Rawpixel.com/Shutterstock, **52–53** Todd Gipstein/National Geographic Creative, **57** Robb Kendrick/National Geographic Creative, **61** © Gregg Segal, **62–63** (c) © Sarah Lee, **63** (br) © Lauren Singer, **65** Rebecca Hale/National Geographic Creative, **66** Cengage Learning, **68** Citizen of the Planet/Alamy Stock Photo, **69** (tc) Arco Images GmbH/Alamy Stock Photo, **72–73** © Pedro Kirilos, **77** Goritza/Shutterstock, **81** © Soma Chakraborty Debnath, **82** (tc) © Wesley Thomas Wong, (tr) © Ali Hamed Haghdoust, (bl) © Debasish Ghosh, (br) © Hiro Kurashina, **85** (t) Matthieu Paley/National Geographic Creative, (br) Cengage Learning, **86** Matthieu Paley/National Geographic Creative, **87** ac_bnphotos/Getty Images, **89** Matthieu Paley/National Geographic Creative, **92–93** (c) © Sasha Martin/Global Table Adventure, **93** (tr) © Sasha Martin/Global Table Adventure, **95** Oliver Hoffmann/Shutterstock, **101** Yuriko Nakao/Reuters, **105** Paper Boat Creative/Getty Images, **106** Kurita Kaku/Getty Images, **109** NASA, **112–113** Stephan Morrell/National Geographic Creative, **114** Stephan Morrell/National Geographic Creative, **121** Wes C. Skiles/National Geographic Creative, **125** Dan Wiklund/Getty Images, **126** petekarici/Getty Images, **128** Burt Silverman/National Geographic Creative, **129** Martin Edström/National Geographic Creative, **132–133** Wes C. Skiles/National Geographic Creative, **134** Alejandro Tumas/National Geographic, **135** Anadolu Agency/Getty Images, **139** Joel Sartore/National Geographic Photo Ark, **141** Michael Wheatley/Alamy Stock Photo, **142–143** John P Kelly/Getty Images, **145** Judith Burrows/Getty Images, **146** Everett Collection, Inc., **149** Adam Gasson/Alamy Stock Photo, **152–153** (t) AP Images/Angela Rowlings, **153** (br) © Glenn Minshall/Northfield Mount Hermon, **157** ZUMA Press, Inc./Alamy Stock Photo, **161** Joel Sartore/National Geographic Photo Ark, **162** Michael Nichols/National Geographic Creative, **165** Mark Thiessen/National Geographic Creative, **166** Lori Epstein/National Geographic Creative, **169** dean bertoncelj/Shutterstock, **172–173** Roy Toft/National Geographic Creative, **173** (tr) Tim Laman/National Geographic Creative, **176** (cl) Andreas Gradin/Shutterstock, (cr) Marina Jay/Shutterstock, **181** Cameron Spencer/Getty Images, **182–183** (c) David Doubilet/National Geographic Creative, **183** (t) James P. Blair/National Geographic Creative, (b) Sisse Brimberg/National Geographic Creative, **185** Beverly Joubert/National Geographic Creative, **186–187** (t) Brent Stirton Images/Getty Images, **187** (tr) © Little Dancer, Aged Fourteen, c.1880–81 (bronze & fabric) (see also 419951–53), Degas, Edgar (1834–1917)/University of East Anglia, Norfolk, UK/Robert and Lisa Sainsbury Collection/Bridgeman Images, (bl) Randy Olson/National Geographic Creative, **188** © Son Truong, **191** Jim Webb/National Geographic Creative, **194–195** (t) Paul Nicklen/National Geographic Creative, **195** (tr) Paul Nicklen/National Geographic Creative, (bl) Paul Nicklen/National Geographic Creative, **196** Paul Nicklen/National Geographic Creative, **199** Peter Essick/National Geographic, **213** Joel van Houdt/National Geographic Creative

Texts/Sources

5–6 Based on information from "Life in a Day: About the Production": http://movies.nationalgeographic.com/movies/life-in-a-day/about-the-production/; **12–13** Based on original interviews with Kakani Katija and Christine Lee, and information from "Ricky Qi: Filmmaker/Photographer": http://www.nationalgeographic.com/explorers/bios/ricky-qi/; **25–26** Based on information from "The First Grader": http://movies.nationalgeographic.com/movies/the-first-grader/; **28** Based on information from "Bound for Marriage as a Child, Now a Change Agent for Kenyan Girls" by Gary Strauss: http://news.nationalgeographic.com/2016/09/kakenya-ntaiya-explorer-moments/; **32–33** Adapted from "Grit Trumps Talent and IQ: A Story Every Parent (and Educator) Should Read" by Marguerite Del Giudice: http://news.nationalgeographic.com/news/2014/10/141015-angela-duckworth-success-grit-psychology-self-control-science-nginnovators/; **45–46** Adapted from "Surviving the Sneaky Psychology of Supermarkets" by Rebecca Rupp: http://theplate.nationalgeographic.com/2015/06/15/surviving-the-sneaky-psychology-of-supermarkets/; **52–53** Based on information from the National Geographic Channel show "Brain Games: The Power of Persuasion";